Everyday Multiculturalisr in/across Asia

What does it mean to bring Asia into conversation with current literature on everyday multiculturalism? This book focuses on the empirical, theoretical and methodological considerations of using an everyday multiculturalism approach to explore the ordinary ways people live together in difference in the Asian region while also drawing attention to increasing trans-Asian mobilities.

The chapters in this collection encompass inter-disciplinary research undertaken in Australia, Hong Kong, Malaysia, Singapore and South Korea that explores some core aspects of everyday multiculturalism as it plays out in and across Asia. These include an increase in intraregional movements and especially labour mobility, which demands regard for the experiences of migrants from Burma, China, Nepal, the Philippines and India; negotiations of cultural diversity in nations where a multi-ethnic citizenry is formally recognised through predominantly pluralist models, and/or where national belonging is highly racialised; and intercultural contestation against, in some cases, the backdrop of a newly emergent multicultural policy environment. The book challenges and reinvigorates discussions around the relative transferability of an everyday multiculturalism framework to Asia, including concepts such as super-diversity, conviviality and everyday racism, and the importance of close attention to how people navigate differences and commonalities in local and trans-local contexts.

This book will be of interest to academics and researchers studying migration, multiculturalism, ethnic and racial studies, and to advanced students of Sociology, Political Science and Public Policy. It was originally published as a special issue of *Ethnic and Racial Studies*.

Jessica Walton researches issues on multiculturalism, identity and racism. Her recent book is titled *Korean Adoptees and Transnational Adoption: Embodiment and Emotion*.

Anita Harris specialises in youth citizenship. Her books include *Young People and Everyday Multiculturalism* and *Future Girl*.

Koichi Iwabuchi works on diversity and cultural citizenship. He is the author of *Resilient Borders and Cultural Diversity: Internationalism, Brand Nationalism, and Multiculturalism in Japan*.

Ethnic and Racial Studies

Series editors: Martin Bulmer, University of Surrey, UK, and John Solomos, University of Warwick, UK

The journal *Ethnic and Racial Studies* was founded in 1978 by John Stone to provide an international forum for high quality research on race, ethnicity, nationalism and ethnic conflict. At the time the study of race and ethnicity was still a relatively marginal sub-field of sociology, anthropology and political science. In the intervening period the journal has provided a space for the discussion of core theoretical issues, key developments and trends, and for the dissemination of the latest empirical research.

It is now the leading journal in its field and has helped to shape the development of scholarly research agendas. *Ethnic and Racial Studies* attracts submissions from scholars in a diverse range of countries and fields of scholarship, and crosses disciplinary boundaries. It is now available in both printed and electronic form. Since 2015 it has published 15 issues per year, three of which are dedicated to *Ethnic and Racial Studies Review* offering expert guidance to the latest research through the publication of book reviews, symposia and discussion pieces, including reviews of work in languages other than English.

The *Ethnic and Racial Studies* book series contains a wide range of the journal's special issues. These special issues are an important contribution to the work of the journal, where leading social science academics bring together articles on specific themes and issues that are linked to the broad intellectual concerns of *Ethnic and Racial Studies*. The series editors work closely with the guest editors of the special issues to ensure that they meet the highest quality standards possible. Through publishing these special issues as a series of books, we hope to allow a wider audience of both scholars and students from across the social science disciplines to engage with the work of *Ethnic and Racial Studies*.

Most recent titles in the series include:

Diaspora Mobilizations for Transitional Justice
Edited by Maria Koinova and Dženeta Karabegović

Everyday Multiculturalism in/across Asia
Edited by Jessica Walton, Anita Harris and Koichi Iwabuchi

Racial Nationalisms
Borders, Refugees and the Cultural Politics of Belonging
Edited by Sivamohan Valluvan and Virinder Kalra

Everyday Multiculturalism in/across Asia

Edited by
**Jessica Walton, Anita Harris
and Koichi Iwabuchi**

Routledge
Taylor & Francis Group

LONDON AND NEW YORK

ETHNIC
◄AND►
RACIAL
STUDIES

First published 2021
by Routledge
2 Park Square, Milton Park, Abingdon, Oxon, OX14 4RN

and by Routledge
52 Vanderbilt Avenue, New York, NY 10017

Routledge is an imprint of the Taylor & Francis Group, an informa business

British Library Cataloguing-in-Publication Data
A catalogue record for this book is available from the British Library

ISBN13: 978-0-367-55281-7

Typeset in Myriad Pro
by codeMantra

Publisher's Note
The publisher accepts responsibility for any inconsistencies that may have arisen during the conversion of this book from journal articles to book chapters, namely the inclusion of journal terminology.

Disclaimer
Every effort has been made to contact copyright holders for their permission to reprint material in this book. The publishers would be grateful to hear from any copyright holder who is not here acknowledged and will undertake to rectify any errors or omissions in future editions of this book.

Contents

Citation Information   vi
Notes on Contributors   viii

Introduction: everyday multiculturalism in/across Asia   1
Jessica Walton, Anita Harris and Koichi Iwabuchi

1   1Malaysia? Young people and everyday multiculturalism in
    multiracialized Malaysia   10
    Anita Harris and Alan Han

2   The limits of "multiculturalism without diversity": multi-ethnic
    students and the negotiation of "difference" in South Korean schools   29
    Jessica Walton

3   Everyday multiculturalism in union: power construction in
    migrant domestic workers' unionism   48
    Raees Begum Baig

4   Multicultural encounters in Singapore's nursing homes: a care
    ethics approach   67
    Shirlena Huang and Brenda S.A. Yeoh

5   Iphones and "African gangs": everyday racism and ethno-
    transnational media in Melbourne's Chinese student world   86
    Fran Martin

6   Humour at work: conviviality through language play in
    Singapore's multicultural workplaces   105
    Amanda Wise and Selvaraj Velayutham

Index   125

Citation Information

The chapters in this book were originally published in the *Ethnic and Racial Studies*, volume 43, issue 5 (February 2020). When citing this material, please use the original page numbering for each article, as follows:

Introduction
Introduction: everyday multiculturalism in/across Asia
Jessica Walton, Anita Harris and Koichi Iwabuchi
Ethnic and Racial Studies, volume 43, issue 5 (February 2020) pp. 807–815

Chapter 1
1Malaysia? Young people and everyday multiculturalism in multiracialized Malaysia
Anita Harris and Alan Han
Ethnic and Racial Studies, volume 43, issue 5 (February 2020) pp. 816–834

Chapter 2
The limits of "multiculturalism without diversity": multi-ethnic students and the negotiation of "difference" in South Korean schools
Jessica Walton
Ethnic and Racial Studies, volume 43, issue 5 (February 2020) pp. 835–853

Chapter 3
Everyday multiculturalism in union: power construction in migrant domestic workers' unionism
Raees Begum Baig
Ethnic and Racial Studies, volume 43, issue 5 (February 2020) pp. 854–872

Chapter 4
Multicultural encounters in Singapore's nursing homes: a care ethics approach
Shirlena Huang and Brenda S.A. Yeoh
Ethnic and Racial Studies, volume 43, issue 5 (February 2020) pp. 873–891

Chapter 5

Iphones and "African gangs": everyday racism and ethno-transnational media in
Melbourne's Chinese student world
Fran Martin
Ethnic and Racial Studies, volume 43, issue 5 (February 2020) pp. 892–910

Chapter 6

Humour at work: conviviality through language play in Singapore's multicul-
tural workplaces
Amanda Wise and Selvaraj Velayutham
Ethnic and Racial Studies, volume 43, issue 5 (February 2020) pp. 911–929

For any permission-related enquiries please visit:
http://www.tandfonline.com/page/help/permissions

Contributors

Raees Begum Baig Department of Social Work, The Chinese University of Hong Kong, Shatin, Hong Kong.

Alan Han Independent Scholar, Toronto, Canada.

Anita Harris Alfred Deakin Institute for Citizenship and Globalisation, Deakin University, Melbourne, Australia.

Shirlena Huang Department of Geography, National University of Singapore, Singapore.

Koichi Iwabuchi School of Sociology, Kwansei Gakuin University, Nishinomiya, Japan.

Fran Martin School of Culture and Communication, The University of Melbourne, Australia.

Selvaraj Velayutham Department of Sociology, Macquarie University, Sydney, Australia.

Jessica Walton Alfred Deakin Institute for Citizenship and Globalisation, Deakin University, Melbourne, Australia.

Amanda Wise Department of Sociology, Macquarie University, Sydney, Australia.

Brenda S.A. Yeoh Department of Geography, National University of Singapore, Singapore.

Introduction: everyday multiculturalism in/across Asia

Jessica Walton ⓘ, Anita Harris ⓘ and Koichi Iwabuchi ⓘ

ABSTRACT
This article introduces the special issue, *Everyday Multiculturalism in/across Asia*. It provides an overview of the international and inter-disciplinary research papers included in the special issue which all speak to the concept of everyday multiculturalism by critically engaging with the extent to which core aspects relate to different contexts in and across Asia. Papers in this collection encompass research undertaken in Australia, Hong Kong, Malaysia, Singapore and South Korea and which include issues of intraregional movement and labour mobility particularly regarding the experiences of migrants from Burma, China, Nepal, The Philippines and India. A key contribution of this special issue is that the papers engage with empirical, theoretical and methodological questions which consider the potential transferability of ideas related to everyday multiculturalism, especially in the context of expanding trans-Asian mobilities.

Introduction

In conversation with current literature on everyday multiculturalism, this special issue on *Everyday Multiculturalism in/across Asia* addresses a significant gap by focusing on empirical, theoretical and methodological considerations in the context of Asian countries while also drawing attention to increasing trans-Asian mobilities. Here, we introduce key themes and contributions from the work included in this special issue. The papers in this collection encompass inter-disciplinary research undertaken in Australia, Hong Kong, Malaysia, Singapore and South Korea that explores some core aspects of everyday multiculturalism as it plays out in and across Asia. These include an increase in intraregional movements and especially labour mobility, which demands regard for the experiences of migrants from Burma, China, Nepal, The Philippines and India; negotiations of cultural diversity in nations where a multi-ethnic citizenry is formally recognized through predominantly pluralist models, and/or where national belonging is highly racialized; and intercultural contestation against, in some cases, the backdrop of a newly emergent multicultural policy environment. An overarching theme that connects the papers is an effort to challenge and reinvigorate discussions around the relative transferability of an everyday multiculturalism framework to Asia, including concepts such as super-diversity, conviviality and everyday racism, and the importance of close attention to how people navigate differences and commonalities in local and trans-local contexts.

Examining "everyday multiculturalism" in/across Asia

This special issue brings together international and interdisciplinary research on everyday multiculturalism with a specific focus on Asian contexts and experiences of living in diversity. The idea for this special issue originated from a two-day invitational workshop held in Melbourne, Australia in October 2016. Presentations and a discussion of full papers included prominent scholars and early career researchers investigating diverse patterns of everyday multiculturalism and trans-Asian mobilities in Asia. To date, the everyday multiculturalism approach has raised important empirical, methodological and ontological questions about how we conceptualize both the "everyday" and what constitutes the kind of working multiculturalism that enables people to live well with difference. Now, however, there is growing interest in the potential transferability of ideas, especially in the context of expanding trans-Asian mobilities. This workshop was held in response to this desire to critically debate the potential use and relevance of everyday multiculturalism to countries across the Asian region, including some foundational concepts such as super-diversity (Vertovec 2007; Wessendorf 2014), conviviality, sociality, and everyday racism, and their application and meaning in different local contexts.

Previously, the majority of research on everyday multiculturalism was conducted in Western contexts, including Australia (Wise 2005, 2009; Wise and Velayutham 2009; Harris 2013; Ho 2011; Lobo 2014; Radford 2016; Noble 2009), the United Kingdom (Amin 2002; Hudson, Phillips, and Ray 2009; Watson 2009; Watson and Saha 2013; Neal et al. 2013; Werbner 2013; Wessendorf 2014), Europe (Colombo and Semi 2007; Räthzel 2008, Frisina 2010), and North America (Radice 2009; Anderson 2011; Han 2009; de Finney 2010; Shan and Walter 2015), often in places where multicultural policy and programmes are well-established. Part of the impetus for an everyday multiculturalism approach in these contexts is the perceived need for increasing attention to how intercultural encounters and "ordinary cosmopolitanism" are operationalized on the ground, outside of these more formal initiatives (and perhaps especially in conditions where a multiculturalism "backlash" is prevalent, see

Vertovec and Wessendorf 2010). This interest in mundane living with difference, especially through "sociability practices" (Glick Schiller, Darieva, and Gruner-Domic 2011, 401), has become an important way to capture the ordinary ways people grapple with diversity beneath and beyond state multiculturalism and state management of migration and settlement. However, it is timely to produce new understandings of diverse forms of everyday multiculturalism outside the West, especially in Asian contexts where multiculturalism is not established policy (Iwabuchi, Kim, and Hsia 2016), or where a state-controlled categorization of multiracialized citizenry is challenged by new migration flows.

Although cultural diversity and migration in the Asian region are certainly not new phenomena, in recent times, countries have been grappling with changing demographics due to increased intraregional migrations, and questions about what it might mean to be a multicultural society have emerged. In some countries, this has sparked national conversations about the implications of migration in terms of multiculturalism. This has emerged in uneven ways, with countries like South Korea taking a top-down approach to multiculturalism policy that selectively focuses on a subset of the population (Kim 2011, 2012), while countries such as Japan, where there is no government multiculturalism policy, nevertheless acknowledge forms of multiculturalism in everyday contexts such as "multicultural co-living" (Iwabuchi, Kim, and Hsia 2016). In countries such as Malaysia and Singapore, rigorous ethnic classification is used to manage the diverse population. Lian (2016, 15) argues that in these post-colonial Asian societies such as Singapore, scholars

> have been more concerned with how multiculturalism is interpreted and used for the purpose of management and government; much less attention is paid to the equally important issue of how people live in essentially multicultural settings and their resistance or accommodation to state management.

However, this shift to an investigation of "how people live in multicultural settings" (Lian 2016, 15) must also be advanced carefully in these contexts where state management of diversity may not look as it does in Australia, the UK, Europe or North America. Cases in East Asia, for example, put into question a tendency of everyday multiculturalism approaches, which, as noted, have been drawn mostly from Euro-American-Australian contexts, to assume particular kinds of policy environments as their backdrops, even while they focus on ordinary intercultural encounters. They pose an intriguing question of whether and how everyday multiculturalism is relevant to the consideration of engagement with the multicultural question in societies where multiculturalism and related immigration and social integration policy have not been well developed on a national level. This does not deny the relevance of everyday multiculturalism in East Asia in terms of mundane experience and negotiation regarding cultural diversity. Yet, to understand the everydayness of multicultural negotiation and engagement in East Asia, it may be more vital to consider how supportive actions in local civil society may have been engendered by the very deficiency of national policy, and accordingly, to establish their potentials (and limitations) to advance multicultural inclusion.

This provocation aligns with a core concern that initial research on everyday multiculturalism aimed to address, namely the relationship between macro and micro levels of multiculturalism. This has often been framed as an inquiry into how people live with and among "difference" in mundane (and extraordinary) ways in familiar contexts (Wise and Velayutham 2009; Neal et al. 2013; Wessendorf 2014), rather than merely focusing on top-down policy approaches to cultural diversity. An emphasis on everyday multiculturalism, however, does not mean that research is only concerned with micro practices with no regard for socio-political context; instead, micro practices are understood in relation to and in the context of macro processes and how these shape and are shaped by everyday interactions: an interconnected loop of structure and agency that is particularly evident in some of the case studies explored in the papers here.

While government policy and political processes clearly matter, not least, as the nation-state determines rights regarding migration and settlement, and still plays a significant role in how racial, ethnic and cultural differences are categorized, acknowledged and addressed, the papers presented here foreground the quotidian experience of living with diversity within these broader conditions. In this respect, they take a different but complementary path from the dominant body of scholarship of multiculturalism and migration in/across Asia, which has tended to emphasize policy context and state actors. The contributors to this special issue highlight the everyday interactions that constitute people's lived experiences in diverse local and trans-local contexts (Greiner and Sakdapolrak 2013) – such as in classrooms and workplaces; streets and public spaces; malls, cafes and commercial sites; civic associations, unions, community groups and other spaces of the public sphere; and social media – that are always shaped by the larger political context.

The contribution of this special issue

The papers in this special issue explore theoretical and methodological considerations for capturing "everyday" practices in different social and cultural Asian contexts where multiculturalism as policy has not been substantially developed and, related to this, how the "experience" of multiculturalism can be localised, contextualized and embodied in ways that are not necessarily spatially and temporally bounded by conventional geographical borders. The papers consider how the particularity of place (including nation, city and field site) matters when considering the transferability and relevance of an everyday multiculturalism framework to Asia. Based on research in Singapore, Australia, Malaysia, South Korea and Hong Kong, this special issue addresses how people's mobility and/or emplacement in different political, cultural and economic Asian contexts shapes and potentially transforms how we conceptualize the lived practice of multiculturalism.

A common theme connecting the papers in this special issue is the everyday interpersonal negotiations and tensions that speak to, against and alongside systemic social and institutionalized racial and ethnic inequities that inform people's everyday realities in relatively diverse contexts. These papers highlight productive forms of resistance as well as mundane social practices that centre on, as well as complicate, friendships, collegial relations and shared city life, and the routinized and unexpected affinities, discordances and connections that flow through these networks of encounter.

Both the paper by Harris and Han (2019) and the paper by Walton (2019) draw attention to an underexplored focus on everyday interactions among children and young people in Malaysia and South Korea, respectively, that reveal how they are affected by top-down government policies that aim to manage racial, ethnic and cultural diversity while also highlighting how they make space for their own negotiations of "difference" that align more with their everyday realities. Harris and Han consider how young Malaysians apprehend and work with formal injunctions to build unity in diversity via the 1Malaysia programme and its legacies, doing so in the context of the persistence of inequitable multiracialism that plays out both structurally and informally. They show how young people's social worlds are simultaneously sites of everyday racism and the reification of racial categories, but at times also enable an everyday cosmopolitanism that problematizes racialization. Although there are hopeful examples in young people's practices, Harris and Han demonstrate that these do not easily overcome institutionalized inequities, especially given they may often invoke other stratifications around class, consumption and mobility. In the context of primary schools in South Korea, Walton examines the strategies multi-ethnic Korean children use to co-exist with their mono-ethnic Korean peers. These are analysed within the context of an exclusionary governmental multiculturalism education policy that serves to marginalize children and their families with multi-ethnic and multi-racial backgrounds, which recognizes and produces their "difference" in order to assimilate their "difference". Although Walton identifies limitations in terms of the extent that multi-ethnic children could challenge or resist the everyday racism and Othering that they experience, this paper highlights how they create spaces to resist and counter exclusionary practices.

The papers by Baig (2019) and Huang and Yeoh (2019) both explore unexpected connections that emerge from trans-Asian mobilities among migrant and local workers. An unexplored area for research on everyday multicultur-alism is examined in Baig's paper on female domestic migrant workers and their interactions with local workers through unionism in Hong Kong. In spite of exclusionary governmental policies relating to migrant domestic workers, the connections that migrant and local domestic workers make in the course of their everyday lives serves to build a sense of interdependence through a commonality that they share centred on workers' rights, which challenges power hierarchies founded on their unequal migration status. In Huang and Yeoh's paper, the framework of a feminist ethics of care is brought to bear to understand the interactions between local and foreign healthcare workers in Singapore as they negotiate their positionalities as care workers in nursing homes in the face of exclusionary policies and insti-tutional practices based on gender, legal status and citizenship. Bringing a focus on the ways different groups "do" care as an under-researched dimen-sion of everyday multiculturalism, their paper examines the boundary-making work that occurs across situations of conflict and cooperation as well as prac-tices of reciprocity (and their limits) in which local and migrant care workers are engaged.

Other papers aim to extend the everyday multiculturalism framework by examining key concepts in new contexts that require a more nuanced analy-sis. Martin's (2019) paper addresses the concepts of super-diversity and every-day multiculturalism in relation to young Chinese women's social media usage in Melbourne, Australia. She argues that these frameworks need to be re-thought when considering the experiences of short-term international stu-dents who have been socialized into a monocultural society and are now encountering everyday life in a super-diverse city. She argues that their experiences and engagements cannot be suitably captured through a frame of hybrid migrant youth culture, which has been used typically to analyse the context of 1.5 and second generation youth who are the main focus of previous research on everyday multiculturalism and super-diversity. She demonstrates how ideas of mundane intercultural encounter in diversity need to account for new modes of youth transnational mobility and local emplacement, as well as attending to mediated youth culture and communi-cations. Similarly, in their paper on humour in Singaporean blue-collar work-places, Wise and Velayutham (2019) consider an under-explored context of everyday multiculturalism that has been produced and shaped by new trans-national mobilities, that of the culturally diverse workplace in a non-Western setting. They show how humour is mobilized as a form of convivial labour that plays with the boundaries of what is considered acceptable when it comes to "ethnic" or "race" joking, and argue that Singlish provides a unique, shared and somewhat neutral template for bridging language play that differentiates it from the affordances of English and its manifestations in Anglo shop-floor humour.

While we have witnessed challenges to multiculturalism, especially as a national discourse, in many Western countries in the last decade (Vertovec and Wessendorf 2010), the discussion of multiculturalism as experienced on the ground, and especially its "lived" dimensions outside of established policy frameworks and beyond flourishing populist nationalism, has been capturing more attention (Valluban 2019). The decay of multiculturalism might not have been a key issue in most Asian countries, but the attention to "lived" multiculture has become no less significant for the consideration of accelerating diversity of Asian countries. This special issue's focus helps us to better understand the effects and implications of trans-Asian mobilities and transient migration that might give rise to post-national, trans-local or highly localised forms of everyday multiculturalism that produce new solidarities and new lines of conflict. It is thus significant for anyone concerned with multiculturalism to make a serious investigation into this emerging phenomenon, and we hope to advance the scholarship on multiculturalism in and across Asia with this special issue.

Disclosure statement

No potential conflict of interest was reported by the authors.

Funding

This work was supported by Australian Research Council [grant number DE160100922].

ORCID

Jessica Walton ⓘ http://orcid.org/0000-0003-3876-2994
Anita Harris ⓘ http://orcid.org/0000-0003-0865-8280
Koichi Iwabuchi ⓘ http://orcid.org/0000-0002-9394-6174

References

Amin, Ash. 2002. "Ethnicity and the Multicultural City: Living with Diversity." *Environment and Planning A: Economy and Space* 34 (6): 959–980.
Anderson, Elijah. 2011. *The Cosmopolitan Canopy: Race and Civility in Everyday Life.* New York: Norton.
Baig, Raees. 2019. "Everyday Multiculturalism in Union: Power Construction in Migrant Domestic Workers' Unionism." *Ethnic and Racial Studies*, this issue.
Colombo, Enzo, and Giovanni Semi. 2007. *Multiculturalismo Quotidiano: Le Pratiche Della Differenza.* Milano: Franco Angeli.
de Finney, Sandrina. 2010. "'We Just Don't Know Each Other': Racialised Girls Negotiate Mediated Multiculturalism in a Less Diverse Canadian City." *Journal of Intercultural Studies* 31 (5): 471–487.

Frisina, Annalisa. 2010. "Young Muslims' Everyday Tactics and Strategies: Resisting Islamophobia, Negotiating Italianness, Becoming Citizens." *Journal of Intercultural Studies* 31 (5): 557–572.

Glick Schiller, Nina, Tsypylma Darieva, and Sandra Gruner-Domic. 2011. "Defining Cosmopolitan Sociability in a Transnational Age. An Introduction." *Ethnic and Racial Studies* 34 (3): 399–418.

Greiner, Clemens, and Patrick Sakdapolrak. 2013. "Translocality: Concepts, Applications and Emerging Research Perspectives." *Geography Compass* 7 (5): 373–384.

Han, Chong-Suk. 2009. "We Both Eat Rice, But That's About It: Korean and Latino Relations in Multi-Ethnic Los Angeles." In *Everyday Multiculturalism*, edited by Amanda Wise, and Selvaraj Velayutham, 237–254. London: Palgrave Macmillan.

Harris, Anita. 2013. *Young People and Everyday Multiculturalism*. New York: Routledge.

Harris, Anita, and Alan Han. 2019. "1Malaysia? Young People and Everyday Multiculturalism in Multiracialised Malaysia." *Ethnic and Racial Studies*, this issue.

Ho, Christina. 2011. "Respecting the Presence of Others: School Micropublics and Everyday Multiculturalism." *Journal of Intercultural Studies* 32 (6): 603–619. doi:10.1080/07256868.2011.618106.

Huang, Shirlena, and Brenda Yeoh. 2019. "Multicultural Encounters in Singapore's Nursing Homes: A Care Ethics Approach." *Ethnic and Racial Studies*, this issue.

Hudson, Maria, Joan Phillips, and Kathryn Ray. 2009. "'Rubbing Along with the Neighbours' — Everyday Interactions in a Diverse Neighbourhood in the North of England." In *Everyday Multiculturalism*, edited by Amanda Wise, and Selvaraj Velayutham, 199–215. London: Palgrave Macmillan.

Iwabuchi, Koichi, Hyun Mee Kim, and Hsiao-Chuan Hsia. 2016. *Multiculturalism in East Asia: A Transnational Exploration of Japan, South Korea and Taiwan*. London: Rowman & Littlefield.

Kim, Joon K. 2011. "The Politics of Culture in Multicultural Korea." *Journal of Ethnic and Migration Studies* 37: 1583–1604.

Kim, Nora Hui-Jung. 2012. "Multiculturalism and the Politics of Belonging: The Puzzle of Multiculturalism in South Korea." *Citizenship Studies* 16 (1): 103–117.

Lian, Kwen Fee. 2016. "Multiculturalism in Singapore: Concept and Practice." In *Multiculturalism, Migration and the Politics of Identity in Singapore*, edited by Kwen Fee Lian, 11–29. Singapore: Springer.

Lobo, Michele. 2014. "Everyday Multiculturalism: Catching the Bus in Darwin, Australia." *Social & Cultural Geography* 15 (7): 714–729. doi:10.1080/14649365.2014.916743.

Martin, Fran. 2019. "iPhones and 'African Gangs': Everyday Racism and Ethnotransnational Media in Melbourne's Chinese Student World." *Ethnic and Racial Studies*, this issue.

Neal, Sarah, Katy Bennett, Allan Cochrane, and Giles Mohan. 2013. "Living Multiculture: Understanding the New Spatial and Social Relations of Ethnicity and Multiculture in England." *Environment and Planning C: Government and Policy* 31 (2): 308–323.

Noble, Greg. 2009. "Everyday Cosmopolitanism and the Labour of Intercultural Community." In *Everyday Multiculturalism*, edited by Amanda Wise, and Selvaraj Velayutham, 46–65. London: Palgrave Macmillan.

Radford, David. 2016. "'Everyday Otherness' – Intercultural Refugee Encounters and Everyday Multiculturalism in a South Australian Rural Town." *Journal of Ethnic and Migration Studies* 42 (13): 2128–2145. doi:10.1080/1369183X.2016.1179107.

Radice, Martha. 2009. "Street-Level Cosmopolitanism: Neighbourhood Shopping in Multi-Ethnic Montreal." In *Everyday Multiculturalism*, edited by Amanda Wise, and Selvaraj Velayutham, 140–157. London: Palgrave Macmillan.

Räthzel, Nora, ed. 2008. *Finding the Way Home: Young People's Stories of Gender, Ethnicity, Class, and Places in Hamburg and London*. Gottingen: V&R Unipress.

Shan, Hongxia, and Pierre Walter. 2015. "Growing Everyday Multiculturalism: Practice-Based Learning of Chinese Immigrants through Community Gardens in Canada." *Adult Education Quarterly* 65 (1): 19–34.

Valluban, Sivamohan. 2019. *The Clamour of Nationalism: Race and Nation in Twenty-First-Century Britain*. Manchester: Manchester University Press.

Vertovec, Steven. 2007. "Super-Diversity and Its Implications." *Ethnic and Racial Studies* 30 (6): 1024–1054.

Vertovec, Steven, and Susanne Wessendorf. 2010. *The Multiculturalism Backlash: European Discourses, Policies and Practices*. London: Routledge.

Walton, Jessica. 2019. "The Limits of 'Multiculturalism without Diversity': Multi-Ethnic Students and the Negotiation of 'Difference' in South Korean Schools." *Ethnic and Racial Studies*, this issue.

Watson, Sophie. 2009. "Brief Encounters of an Unpredictable Kind: Everyday Multiculturalism in Two London Street Markets." In *Everyday Multiculturalism*, edited by Amanda Wise, and Selvaraj Velayutham, 125–139. London: Palgrave Macmillan.

Watson, Sophie, and Anamik Saha. 2013. "Suburban Drifts: Mundane Multiculturalism in Outer London." *Ethnic and Racial Studies* 36 (12): 2016–2034. doi:10.1080/01419870.2012.678875.

Werbner, Pnina. 2013. "Everyday Multiculturalism: Theorising the Difference between 'Intersectionality' and 'Multiple Identities.'" *Ethnicities* 13 (4): 401–419.

Wessendorf, Susanne. 2014. *Commonplace Diversity: Social Relations in a Super-Diverse Context*. Basingstoke: Palgrave MacMillan.

Wise, Amanda. 2005. "Hope and Belonging in a Multicultural Suburb." *Journal of Intercultural Studies* 26 (1-2): 171–186.

Wise, Amanda. 2009. "Everyday Multiculturalism: Transversal Crossings and Working Class Cosmopolitans." In *Everyday Multiculturalism*, edited by Amanda Wise, and Selvaraj Velayutham, 21–45. London: Palgrave Macmillan.

Wise, Amanda, and Selvaraj Velayutham, eds. 2009. *Everyday Multiculturalism*. London: Palgrave MacMillan.

Wise, Amanda, and Selvaraj Velayutham. 2019. "Humour at Work: Conviviality through Language Play in Singapore's Multicultural Workplaces." *Ethnic and Racial Studies*, this issue.

1Malaysia? Young people and everyday multiculturalism in multiracialized Malaysia

Anita Harris and Alan Han

ABSTRACT

In Malaysia over the last decade, a more meaningful form of multiculturalism beyond mere tolerance has been encouraged through the 1Malaysia initiative of the Najib government. This paper explores how a framework of everyday multiculturalism can enhance our understanding of the ways Malaysian youth negotiate formal injunctions to build unity in diversity while an inequitable multiracialism persists both structurally and informally in Malaysian society. We illustrate how an everyday multiculturalism approach reveals on-the-ground processes of the (re)production of unequal difference and ordinary possibilities for interethnic conviviality.

Introduction

In 2009, the then Malaysian Government introduced the 1Malaysia (1M) programme to encourage Malaysians – especially youth – to learn about and respect each other's cultures. According to its website (http://www. 1malaysia.com.my/en), its objective is "unity in diversity and inclusiveness ... accepting and celebrating our differences, not mere tolerance or respect". 1Malaysia encouraged a deeper form of multiculturalism beyond mere tolerance to develop a more inclusive national image and increase collaborative economic productivity for a global economy. However, during the early era of 1Malaysia and even with a recent change in government, a pluralist national identity has remained the paradigm, and there is considerable scepticism amongst youth about top-down efforts to promote mixing and celebration of difference while an inequitable multiracialism persists both structurally and informally in Malaysian society.

In this paper we explore how a framework of everyday multiculturalism can enhance our understanding of the ways Malaysian youth negotiate these formal injunctions to build unity in diversity and celebrate multiracialism. We consider how longstanding, institutionalized stratifications around race, ethnicity and religion affect young people's everyday social practices and friendships, how they devise their own ways of negotiating and complicating difference and managing conflict, and how they deal with unequal difference in pragmatic ways. We suggest that rhetorical, state-led efforts such as 1Malaysia sit in complex relation with these everyday realities. We show how young people's social worlds are sites of everyday racism and the reification of racial categories, but can also produce an everyday cosmopolitanism that cuts through a racialized paradigm. Even so, youth practices do not easily overcome institutionalized inequities that remain entrenched in the pluralist discourse of unity, and further, they may in turn invoke other stratifications around class, consumption and mobility. We argue for the value of an everyday multiculturalism approach to a place such as Malaysia in order to understand on-the-ground processes of the (re)production of unequal difference and ordinary possibilities for interethnic conviviality.

Multiracialism in Malaysia

Malaysia has always been multicultural, even before it became a nation. The Malay Peninsula was a trading port for traders from India and China between the fourteenth and eighteenth centuries, functioning as a gateway between Asia and the West on Arabic and Chinese trading routes. During this time the area was colonized by the Portuguese, the Dutch, and the British, adding further layers to its rich social and cultural life. Today, although Malaysia is often represented as "a multicultural, multiracial society with no 'real' majority" (Tamam 2013, 86), Malays constitute the majority numerically and politically, while the Chinese are economically dominant and Indians the most disadvantaged (Tamam 2013, 86). According to government statistics, 68.6 per cent of Malaysians are Bumiputera or "sons of soil" (including around 63 per cent Malay Muslims [Joseph 2014, 3] and Indigenous and others), 23.4 per cent are Chinese, 7 per cent Indian and 1 per cent Others; 10.3 per cent of the population is made up of non-citizens (Department of Statistics Malaysia 2017). Racial or ethnic categories are defined in categorical and unique ways in Malaysia and race constitutes an official and singular identity for its citizens (it is important to note that "race" and "ethnicity" are often used interchangeably, see Khoo 2014). Malaysia's multiculturalism is best described as pluralist, and has an internal hierarchy. As Ang (2010, 7) outlines,

> in the Malaysian context, peaceful co-existence is assumed to depend on keeping ethnic group identities distinct and their respective rights clearly demarcated, with the continuing central authority and symbolic dominance of the Malays explicitly sanctioned and unchallenged.

Malaysian multiculturalism cannot be understood without some background of its colonial history (see Noor and Leong 2013, 714). Racial segregation was established in both the colonial and post-colonial periods in the form of race-based schools, racialized labour markets, and spatial separation via the establishment of gated villages and enclaves for different ethnic groups (see Koh 2017). Under British rule, essentialized ethnic groups were segregated into different economic sectors, education systems and geographical areas, with Malays relegated to the peasant sector. Consequently,

> the task for postcolonial Malaysia was not so much one of recognising cultural difference and valuing cultural diversity within an already existing liberal nation-state, but the more urgent one of creating a workable new nation-state out of a plural multi-ethnic society which was the legacy of colonial British rule. (Ang 2010, 4; see also Gabriel 2015)

Independence from Britain was secured in 1957 by an alliance of ethnic-group-based political parties under a power-sharing arrangement. Political compromise amongst these groups resulted in special rights for Bumiputera in education and the public service being enshrined in the Constitution. In exchange, Chinese and Indians were granted citizenship rights and freedom to pursue economic activities (Joseph 2014, 32). However, economic inequality, civil unrest (including 1969's so-called racial riots) and struggles over political power saw this system challenged, and resulted in the Malay-dominated alliance implementing widespread affirmative action policies for Malays under the rubric of the New Economic Policy (Noor and Leong 2013, 717), which included access to higher education via scholarships and quota systems, preferential award of government contracts, regulations around businesses and loans, and policies promoting the hegemonic representation of Malay and Islamic culture (Joseph 2014, 37). Throughout the 2000s, interethnic tensions rose as a result of these economic development plans and nation-building projects that instituted growing racialization and Islamisation (Khoo 2009, 89).

As part of a new set of reforms and policy initiatives in 2009, Malaysia's then recently instated Prime Minister Najib Tun Razak introduced 1Malaysia, which was designed to moderate these affirmative action policies and improve economic growth. 1Malaysia is made up of a series of initiatives, including programmes to enhance unity across difference, inclusiveness and fairness, and the implementation of services and government investments to improve economic performance. According to its website, 1Malaysia is "a concept that encapsulates the very idea of unity in diversity, and … the importance of national unity regardless of race, background, or religious belief" (1Malaysia 2018). Ang (2010, 7) suggests that this "more integrative vision has been proposed over time to respond to changes in society and as Malaysia inserts itself into a globalised capitalist modernity" – in particular, it is a response to a perceived need for a more unified, inclusive and cosmopolitan national identity to better brand the nation and maximize opportunities in a global capitalist economy, including international tourism and investment.

This shift in national image has had some desired effects, especially for external branding, and indeed many scholars note how it dovetails with the successful tourism campaign "Malaysia, Truly Asia", which depicts Malaysia as a globally engaged multiracial nation where several distinct Asian cultures harmoniously co-exist (Ang 2010; Gabriel 2015). However, 1Malaysia leaves unchallenged the dominant, separationist discourse of race and the colonially constructed "plural-society" paradigm (Gabriel 2015, 795). It promotes togetherness and celebration of difference, but also persists in institutionalising multiracialism. It may also have deepened internal divisions and failed to result in institutional reforms, in large part because the state has not been able to appease opposing groups (see Noor and Leong 2013, 719; Koh 2015). Indeed, such disenchantment has led to widespread trans-ethnic activism, resulting in the end of 60 years of Barisan Nasional rule at the 2018 election.

Everyday multiculturalism

Even while the state has established formal programmes for a harmonious, racialized plurality, an "everyday multiculturalism" also operates in Malaysia, manifest in the routine and mundane (re)production of racial difference and racism, practices, spaces and moments of conviviality, and opportunities for non-racialized individual and collective identities at the grassroots level. Everyday multiculturalism is taken to mean lived experiences of diversity and practices of relating to difference in ordinary spaces of encounter (see Wise and Velayutham 2009, 3). It draws attention to mundane forms of sociality amidst concerns about rising ethnic tensions and the failure of multicultural and migration policy (especially in the West), while not retreating from analysis of everyday conflict and discord. Indeed, a focus on everyday racism is integral to an everyday multiculturalism approach, for it addresses the whole spectrum of intercultural relations at the local level (Wise and Velayutham 2009, 8). As Wise and Noble (2016, 425) write, "studies of the everyday have the capacity to understand both everyday racism and everyday cosmopolitanism … as coexisting, as not mutually exclusive". For our purposes, everyday multiculturalism as a frame is especially useful because it captures not only informal and mundane practices of cosmopolitanism (that is, openness, sociability and conviviality) but the ordinary (re)production of difference that undergirds both public rhetoric about division *and* political programmes of unity. In the Malaysian context, an investigation of everyday multiculturalism uncovers the tensions and possibilities in interethnic mix that exist alongside formal calls for harmony and may not fit neatly into governmental ideals of multiracialized togetherness. It reveals how ordinary people actively produce and contest racial categories and interethnic relations that illustrate persistent racialized, institutionalized inequities that the state may not acknowledge.

Everyday multiculturalism is also valuable to our analysis because it does not simply provide an ethnographic dimension to contact theory by examining how diverse people engage across their differences, but offers a more critical approach to theorisation of difference in the first place. Rather than taking racial, ethnic or cultural categories as pre-given and fixed, an everyday multiculturalism approach attends to the ways these are made meaningful and habitable through particular political histories and structures of ethnic governance, and then animated and negotiated in the space of encounter. As Semi et al. (2009, 67) argue, the frame of everyday multiculturalism draws attention to "the recurrent situations" in which difference is "constructed, invoked, mediated, transformed, disputed or deconstructed". Race, for example, is not pre-existent material that is a property of an individual and then brought to an encounter with others, but functions as a politically constructed category that is (re)produced and deployed in situated action. In Malaysia, as we have noted, racial difference is institutionalized, racialized inequities are sanctioned, and there is little formal public discourse about racism, not least owing to sedition laws. Race operates as a foundational category of classification and governmentality that appears everywhere in the form of an apparently neutral and stable descriptor. As Gabriel (2015, 783) notes, race (or ethnicity) is a fundamental organising principle: written into policies, embedded in the state's institutions, and inscribed formally into one's identity, with birth certificates and national identity cards classifying all Malaysians into one of four possible racial categories: "Malay", "Chinese", "Indian", or "Other" (MCIO). The frame of everyday multiculturalism can enable us to see how these politically inscribed categories are brought to life, constructed and sometimes disrupted in daily social practice.

In the next section of this paper we seek to explore how interethnic relations amongst youth of the Najib era play out and how difference is constituted and at times complicated in the everyday, alongside 1Malaysia's implicit injunction to maintain multiracialism by building unity in diversity and celebrating difference. We are particularly concerned with the tensions between ideals of harmonious multiracialism, which presume fixed categories and taken-for-granted hierarchies of race, and the relational production of unequal difference through everyday racism (as well as its disruption through productive mix and potentially more fluid experience of diverse identities) that an everyday multiculturalism approach reveals. We demonstrate how these everyday social relations illustrate the ordinary production of racial categorisation and separatism through processes of racism *and* conviviality, and are also an important site for reflexivity, contestation and sometimes the practice of more cosmopolitan ways of being.

About the study

This paper draws on data from a project entitled "Young People and Social Inclusion in the Multicultural City", led by Harris. The purpose of the study was to understand young people's perceptions and experiences of intercultural relations, including barriers and enablers regarding mix, with particular attention to the different demographic, cultural and policy environments of some key multicultural sites in Australia, Europe and Asia. One component of the project involved in-depth interviews undertaken between 2010 and 2012 (during the Najib administration at the height of "1Malaysia") with 15 students aged 21–25 of diverse backgrounds at a major public university in Kuala Lumpur, Malaysia. Participants were recruited via a lecturer, who advertised the project to her English Literature students, some of whom then volunteered to participate. Although there was no attempt to obtain a representative sample, the participants reflected the ethnic and religious diversity of Malaysia's population. According to their self-descriptions, four were Malay Muslim, two Chinese Buddhist, one Chinese Christian, two Chinese-Indian Catholic, two Indian Hindu, one Punjabi Sikh, one Telugu Hindu and two Sri Lankan/Ceylonese Hindu. Twelve participants were female and three male. Some limitations include the small sample size, and the convenience sampling approach, which meant that participants were from the same course (Arts) which may have pre-disposed them to openness to difference and mix.

Interviews covered a range of topics regarding multiculturalism policy, everyday interethnic interactions, views on ethnic groups, inclusion and racism, as well as more general discussion of youth social lives, leisure practices and everyday activities. Participants also drew maps of places they spent time and places they avoided. All interviews were undertaken in English by Han, who occupied an insider/outsider position as an Australian of Chinese ancestry born in Malaysia. Interview material was coded in NVivo and analysed according to key themes that emerged across the larger project as well as within this site-specific study.

1Malaysia and everyday multiracialism

Young people's reception of the 1Malaysia initiative demonstrated a gap between formal policy and programmes and everyday realities. Amongst the participants there was support for the principles that 1Malaysia espouses, such as respect for difference and especially the notion that Malaysia's economic and cultural strength should come from unity in diversity and harnessing the potential of the three major ethnic groups to work together. However, they expressed scepticism about 1Malaysia as a programme that could or would implement change, given deeper structural issues of segregation, with some perceiving it as rhetoric or "branding" that did not reflect or respond to everyday conditions of racialized co-living. For example, Sophie (female, Malay Muslim) said:

> Is it wrong if I say it didn't have any effect? ... It's a government plan or something ... just to bring all the indigenous, Chinese, Malay, Indian together. I think it did work on TV ... You can see in Malaysian advertisements, you can see a lot of 1Malaysia thingy and blah, blah, blah ... So, what is 1Malaysia? For me it's just that ... you're mixed ... with Chinese, Indian. Basically that's it. If they all quarrel with each other they will still quarrel, right? The problem is that if you're a Malay, you'll have the tendency to communicate or interact with a Malay. We have ... Malay schools, Chinese schools, Indian schools, Penang schools. So it's hard to find a Malay who is a friend with Chinese ... in terms of hanging out, or ... sharing problems ... girl stuff, it's probably a Malay will prefer a Malay, a Chinese will prefer a Chinese.

For Sophie, 1Malaysia is an advertising slogan that merely describes the diversity of the population. Although purporting to bring ethnic groups together, simply describing the ethnic mix or prescribing togetherness does not address underlying ethnic divisions or lack of deep connection. As Sophie indicates, structural segregation, such as exists in the Malaysian school system, militates against more meaningful interaction, with knock-on effects that delimit interpersonal relationships that are the foundation for trust, mutuality and care: enabling conditions for deep interculturality. Such affects and ethics can be built through shared participation in institutional and associational life (Wise 2009; Amin 2002; Harris 2013), but these opportunities are lost through institutionalized separation of ethnic groups in Malaysia's racially segregated education system where each ethnic group attends its "own" school and receives instruction in only its "own" language (Koh 2017; Joseph 2014).

Others were even more explicit in their view that 1Malaysia was failing to effect change in interethnic relations because it sidestepped the issue of institutionalized segregation that undercuts efforts for everyday engagement. Esmeralda (female, Sri Lankan Hindu) spoke about the spatially separated ethnic enclaves that are a legacy of a colonial racial-spatial order (for example, the forced relocation of groups of Chinese into guarded villages under colonial rule during the Malayan Emergency; see Koh 2017):

> 1M pisses me off – my friends and I always mock it because we're the real 1M and we've never branded ourselves as that. We also only see ourselves as a group of friends; we don't think, "look at us, we're a Chinese/Malay/Indian!" We disagree with 1M because it's a lie; it's trying to promote Malaysian people as united but when you look at the way we live, it's actually so segregated ... There are different areas in which Chinese live in one place and the Malay live separately. There are exceptions: my upbringing, my friends and I, our social network, you can see how multicultural we truly are ... I think it has to do with class as well. I tend to notice that poorer people stick to their own

race. The richer and educated people seem to understand, to go beyond racial barriers.

Esmeralda identifies spatial separation of ethnic neighbourhoods as a core problem for productive multiculturalism, describing her mixed social network as an exception. She also alludes to a kind of (elite) cosmopolitanism amongst young people such as her friendship group, and suggests that this kind of group is "the real 1M". They do not superficially brand or identify themselves as a culturally mixed group, but develop friendships across ethnicity that can be more authentic because they acknowledge segregation and inequity. Suggesting that this propensity may be more evident amongst those who are well-educated and wealthy hints at a link between class, some manifestations of cosmopolitanism and the emergence of a global youth elite that we revisit later.

Other participants echoed the view that slogans like 1M bear little resemblance to ethnic relations on the ground, where interventions and programmes within families, neighbourhoods and schools to support communication, anti-racism and engagement were sorely needed in the context of the colonial legacy of spatially segregated ethnic communities. For example, Shi (female, Indian-Sri Lankan Hindu) said:

> 1M will work if it starts from young; they should start from preschool and school and family members, particularly the parents, should start it at home. Get their kids to mingle with their neighbours who are from different cultures ... Do not brand those neighbours ... Then in schools, teachers should not be ... biased ... Then this 1Malaysia thing will work.

As Aziz, Ismail, and Yazid (2013, 42) have argued, while 1Malaysia involves the provision of some amenity and services, such as medical clinics and shops, and also more banal cosmo-nationalism such as theme songs, there have been "only minimal efforts made at ethnic integration using the environmental aspect", that might begin to ameliorate some of these everyday divisions and enhance mixing through the sharing of space and the development of mutual attachment to place. Aziz et al. note that initiatives that bring neighbours, families and young people together, such as community gardens and play areas, are amongst the most important environmental changes that improve the frequency and quality of interethnic contact (see also Wise 2009). Given the absence of such practical initiatives, it is not surprising that 1M was often perceived with cynicism amongst youth (see also Lim 2013; Ooi 2015).

Everyday racism

Discussions of 1Malaysia also triggered strong responses because the concept was perceived to paper over the everyday reality of young people's lives wherein difference, inequities and conflict were constantly made present. As indicated, the segregated nature of schools and neighbourhoods inculcated scepticism about unity in diversity (see also Daniels 2010). Other public and formal spaces where racial categories, hierarchies, divisions and inequities are inscribed included shops and public transport. This was illustrated by Esmeralda (female, Sri Lankan Hindu), who indicated that racial signifiers took precedence over other forms of self- and other-identification and were deployed in order to contend with the racialized hierarchy that operates in public spaces:

> It's apparent in public spaces also; say you're an Indian and you go into a shop and there is an Indian salesperson, they'll inquire with the Indian and avoid the Malay or Chinese salesperson … Not that they'll avoid the other person but they'll gravitate towards their own people.

Having a clear sense of who one's "people" were structured social interactions in public spaces. This involved a process of actively producing clear racial categories so that social life could proceed according to the implicit rules of the unequal multiracial order. For example, those with indeterminate ethnicity had to strategize in order to be "read" in the most positive way when they engaged with others in public. Michelle (female, Chinese-Indian Catholic), who was "mixed race", said:

> You can't tell what ethnicity I am when you see me because sometimes I look Malaysian or Indian and sometimes Chinese. When I speak in English I'm charged more, when I speak in Malay like a Malay then it's ok and I'm able to cover my true identity. When I go to a Chinese shop I'm stuck because I can't speak Mandarin or anything so I speak in Bahasa and I'm charged more. When I go to an Indian shop the same happens because they think I look Chinese. So it's everywhere for me. But I can try to use language as a strategy to avoid this sometimes because of my skin colour.

Indeed, although the research used a convenience sample, it is striking that the somewhat random group of participants included many whose racial, cultural, ethnic and religious identifications were very mixed and did not neatly line up with Malaysia's rigid MCIO classification system. Experiences such as Michelle's, of being "misrecognized" or strategically enacting different racial identities depending on the circumstances, were not uncommon. This reveals the way race is actively and reflexively produced by individuals in consequential encounters structured by social expectations of categorical identities. It also indicates how there is little space in the politics of multiracialism for the recognition of diversity and hybridity within identities in spite of the common and widespread "mixedness" of Malaysians. In this instance, multilingualism as a manifestation of hybridity can only function as a momentary strategy for overcoming disadvantage rather a celebrated expression of Malaysian cosmopolitanism.

Public incidents of separatism, exclusion and discrimination were under-scored by various forms of everyday racism amongst peers. This often took the form of "teasing" and belittling. For example, Arnab (female, Punjabi Sikh) said:

> A Sikh is supposed to have a turban … but … it's difficult to maintain your culture because of teasing … My cousins have been bullied because they have turbans. … But this is life in Malaysia and you have to accept how it is. I think racism in Malaysia happens all the time and that it's something we can't avoid. It happens a lot to Indians especially; they're looked down on, are bad-mouthed, and fights happen … If we say that it doesn't happen then that's a lie.

Natalin (female, Chinese Buddhist) said: "Religion is quite big; it can cause fights especially when people aren't tolerant. For example, Muslims will laugh at us for praying to dolls and we will make jokes about them kissing the floor".

Indeed, for most, racism was seen as a critical issue in Malaysia that was only compounded by what were perceived to be efforts to conceal or down-play it via superficial "branding" messages of unity. Michelle (female, Chinese-Indian Catholic) described this as the "show" versus the real "issues":

> It might be nice for a foreigner or tourist to see that there are many different people here with different skin colours but that's about it. It's just a showcase, a surface level … New arrivals aren't aware of the issues here.

As these comments imply, entreaties to "tolerance" and its function as a pro-tective factor against racism, or celebrations of difference for marketing pur-poses, sat in uneasy relation to the divisions and exclusions these young people identified that lie beneath the surface and were ever-present in their everyday lives.

Formal spaces of integration

There were however formal efforts and spaces for ethnic integration that several felt went some way towards enhancing tolerance and togetherness in spite of segregation and racism. One example is the (now scrapped) national service programme of compulsory national training camps for ran-domly selected high school graduates, explicitly implemented by the then government to encourage racial tolerance and national pride amongst youth. As Jane (female, Chinese-Indian Catholic) said:

> National service was a program introduced by the government to enhance harmony. For me, national service has made a difference … We were all forced to speak Bahasa. Because each group has its own language, the one thing that's supposed to unite us all is that we speak Bahasa. So it did unite us, as we were forced to speak a common language. We were also all housed together; we were very mixed. But you also need to have the right spirit, to go in saying that yes, you want to make a change and want to come out different and truly feel 1M.

Jane had a positive experience of national service creating a sense of unity through shared language, purpose and living quarters (see also Ahmad et al. 2013), but she indicates that the "right spirit" is also necessary to realize a sense of shared belonging. Again, she suggests a gap between the 1M ideology and people's capacity to "truly feel" togetherness, which can only be bridged by acknowledging a need to "make a change" and a preparedness to "come out different". The formal imposition of "unity" and forced togetherness were not necessarily discounted, but could only engender meaningful change in ethnic relations and national identity if people were committed to shifting attitudes. Moreover, the national service programme as a manifestation of the 1M agenda underscored togetherness in difference and nationalism without necessarily altering assumptions about the fixed nature of racial groupings. It has been widely criticized for its ideological function and has since been dumped by the new government.

University was another commonly perceived example of a formal space of integration (even while most universities are still ethnically divided), and for some, was especially important after a very segregated school experience. For example, Abidin (male, Malay Muslim) said:

> Young people at school are still divided into races. They … don't develop different perceptions about other races. University is different …. Coming to University has allowed me to develop an understanding about different people because there are different races, different backgrounds, and different religions. We integrate and communicate together because we study our degrees and follow the same rules. I ask people questions and learn a lot about their culture … I helped organise the Mooncake Festival with the Chinese and learnt why they celebrate it. Friends also ask me about my culture.

And Shi (female, Sri Lankan Hindu) described positive mixing amongst students at her university based on her experience of being an "Indian" student representative, getting together with other ethnic representatives and creating programmes:

> I was a student rep … I represented Indians. I had this Chinese friend who represented the Chinese students. We would sit and laugh around. We tried to discuss what we should do for our students. That was a social, intermingling session.

However, there was some indication that the integration and mixing that took place was rather institutionalized, and still based on the foregrounding of categorical racial difference brought together for cultural exchange. These everyday social experiences of mixing simultaneously reveal the ordinary production of racial categorisation through processes of conviviality. Tamam and Krauss (2017, 141) note that interethnic contact is often strongly promoted at public universities through activities that do foster greater intercultural sensitivity. However, such programmes for integration do not enable identities to be "shifted and opened up" and "sometimes mutually reconfigured in the process" (Wise 2009, 23), as per a deeper and more critical kind of mixing, but require young people to inhabit, perform and reify rigid racial identities. While these experiences were often personally rewarding for the young people in our research, they did not necessarily facilitate critical reflection on racialisation, the recognition of inequity, or offer strategies to challenge these issues.

Everyday cosmopolitanism

Alongside these more formal examples of programmes and institutional environments where young people were encouraged to mix, many participants indicated the more informal, everyday ways in which they crossed differences. Taste-based relationships and youth culture were important in connecting young people in ways that were seen to either transcend ethnicity or enable it to be encountered less problematically. As Ferrarese (2014) has argued in relation to young Malaysians in music subcultures, "ethnic identities are refigured to some extent and transcended through scene identifications". When asked what brought together young people of different backgrounds, Mimi (female, Chinese Buddhist) responded,

> Similar interests; for example, in my group, all of us like branded things like iPad and iPhone. The same interests mix us together. So we go shopping and prefer the same brand, we have the same taste on how to dress ourselves, we like the same dress, the same concerts.

These activities were important enablers of togetherness. Misake (female, Indian Hindu) said "I have one Chinese friend and one Malay friend. We are the ones who always hang together even for eat sushi or run – going shopping. It's kind of fun, and you always have a … '1Malaysia'!"

Similarly, Sha (female, Telugu Hindu) said:

> I have friends with different cultural backgrounds; I have very close Malay friends … Sometime we meet up and usually meet at KFC or McDonalds and have a seat and talk.

There has been some considerable work on the ways youth culture and consumption facilitate such "border crossing" (Thomas and Butcher 2003; Nayak 2003; Harris 2013), including the role of consumer spaces and products that are "modern" or Western. Jones et al. (2015, 646) argue that chains like McDonalds perform an important function as a space of inclusion in culturally diverse areas, as their offerings are familiar owing to their massive multinational reach, they are sufficiently "unmarked" by any local culture to be apprehended equally by all, and thus "are in place but not of place, expressing corporate versions of cosmopolitanism" (Jones et al. 2015, 651).

In places such as Malaysia, the venues where multi-ethnic young people meet up, and especially the places they eat, need to be neutral in order that the whole mixed social group is able to participate while being seen to uphold their ethno-religious identities. Further, as Khoo (2009, 89) notes, such "spatial possibilities for commensality have shrunk with growing racialization and Islamisation which rigidly divide Malaysians into Muslim and non-Muslim, and drive non-Muslim eating places to adapt to and conform to a halal economy". Mimi (female, Chinese Buddhist) illustrated this challenge:

> My group of friends and I went to a shopping mall and my Chinese friend wanted pork for lunch but my Malay friend couldn't eat pork and so my friend suggested that whoever wanted pork could stay at the restaurant and the others can leave. My Malay friends weren't happy about it and they seldom talk to each other or hang out any more. This is a rare occasion. Because we live in Malaysia we know that their religion restricts them from eating pork and so we must learn to be a little more understanding. We should have gone to a Western street so that everybody can sit down and eat.

While eating at a "Western street" may have enabled inclusion via the kind of corporate-facilitated cosmopolitanism outlined above, at the same time, as Khoo (2009) suggests, participation in Western/modern consumer culture demands language skills and cultural capital that many youth do not possess. Implied in participants' discussion of consumption as a way to cross difference, is that class cuts across capacity to engage in activities such as eating together at Western restaurants or sharing the enjoyment of purchasing and playing together on expensive branded electronic devices, as mentioned by several participants. Further, there is a dearth of non-consumer spaces for young people to mix across ethnic boundaries and share leisure interests such as playing music together or other activities of production and creation that do not wholly rely on purchasing and consuming. While some such opportunities exist virtually (see Lim 2013), as noted by Ferrarese (2014), without physical and non-commercial spaces for young people to come together for shared leisure interests, multi-ethnic and especially multi-class Malaysian youth communities that can disrupt unequal multiracialism and enable new solidarities are likely to remain fragile.

It is also important to note that for these Malaysian youth, class not only relates to economic status, but is bound up in particular modalities of situating oneself in time and space; being from the "right" geographical locale, in particular the city, and having the "right" contemporary rather than "backward" disposition were seen as important ingredients for (elite) cosmopolitanism. This is consistent with Salleh's (2013) research, which reveals that urban youth are more likely than rural to identify as Malaysian (over local or ethnic identities) and claim to be proud of cultural diversity. The somewhat elusive quality of being "modern" or having a "city" mindset was one way that some participants tried to capture a propensity for cosmopolitanism amongst their social group, along with this interest in (and means for) consumption. In this respect, a capacity for everyday cosmopolitanism that transcended more formal efforts to engender togetherness was closely tied to ideas about urban lifestyle, modern attitudes and new formations of the youthful middle class. For example, Arnab (female, Punjabi Sikh) said "On campus, most of my friends are city girls; we are probably friends because we have the same mindset or because we were all brought up in the city". And Natalin (female, Chinese Buddhist) mentioned that she was able to get along well with an Indian friend because she "is quite modern-thinking and so there are no barriers with her", which she contrasted with the interests of another girl who liked "the Indian type of stuff", taken to mean more "traditional", and thus "there might be a bit of difference in taste and stuff".

As Joseph (2014, 191) has argued, young women in particular are caught in conflicting modes of being Malaysian. While in some ways the young women in her research were able to "transcend cultural and ethnic boundaries and draw on multiple cultural markers in their ways of being", this was often through association with a global "modern" consumer culture that required considerable resources for participation. Similarly, some of the young women in our research also indicated that one way to produce themselves as a modern "new generation of transcultural Malaysians" was to draw on resources and representations of the neoliberal capitalist subject (see Harris 2004). Notions of being a "city" girl or having "modern thinking" could be code for this kind of subjectivity. We can also recall here Esmeralda's comments about her own "1Malaysia" social group, perhaps made up of these kinds of young women, and better understand her reflection that this elite cosmopolitanism is only possible amongst those of a certain class status, and why it might be that she felt that "the richer and educated people seem to understand, to go beyond racial barriers".

Everyday pragmatics

We have indicated that young people's forms of everyday multiculturalism can be institutionalized through formal spaces and enacted through youth cultures of "cosmopolitan consumption", which may engender other hierarchies around class and social mobility. Young people also engaged in an everyday pragmatics that allowed them to achieve a sense of belonging, develop social bonds with those of other ethnicities, and navigate the sensitive terrain of racialized inequities by maintaining reflexivity about their interethnic practice. Rather than pretending that unity exists, or conversely, speaking in too explicit and divisive ways about these matters (and thereby also risking formal censure), many young people maintain good relations by deliberately avoiding sensitive topics. When asked what it was to "be Malaysian", Mary (female, Chinese Christian) said:

Someone who knows what it's like to live in a country where there are issues about race; racism is not outwardly portrayed but more insidious. So to be a Malaysian you need to know where to step and where to push for rights. There is always an invisible line you try not to cross ... I did have Indian and Malay friends in in high school but we wouldn't talk about religion ... In Malaysia we have a lot of sensitive issues that we try not to touch on; things regarding religion and race.

Similarly, Sha (female, Telugu Hindu) spoke of avoiding certain topics to maintain good relations, especially with those who may have power over her employment opportunities:

We have our limits amongst us; we don't talk bad about them and they don't talk bad about us and there are certain topics we don't discuss ... At the end of the day I'll want to work in a government or public companies which are mostly run by Malays ... My friends and I have our cultural issues but we don't talk about them ... we respect each other and our friendship and so we don't talk badly of each other's cultures.

Misake (female, Indian Hindu) also underscored the need to keep quiet about some issues for the sake of maintaining friendships:

As I was born in Malaysia and have grown up here I feel comfortable and at home and have a lot of freedom. If I moved to another country I'd feel uneasy and out of place. Malaysia is OK as long as you don't bring up the sensitive issues. There are limited opportunities in education and the workforce available to people who aren't Malay; it doesn't affect friendships and relationships with other people as long as we don't touch on this sensitive issue. For example, with my Malay friends we would avoid the topic because we don't want any misunderstanding. We just keep quiet, it's better than ruining a friendship.

The avoidance of sensitive topics is about both keeping one's prospects intact, and ensuring smooth-running friendships. Possibly, those who have the most at stake are at the forefront of maintaining good relations with others and must do this difficult emotional work of keeping "nice"; for example, Tamam (2013, 93) demonstrates that Indian students drive the (still limited) "interracial bridging" that occurs amongst young people at university, whereas this is engaged in least by Malays. However, Misake's efforts were also about enhancing her own feelings of being comfortable and "in place". Along with Mary, she suggests that to be Malaysian, to feel a sense of national belonging, may mean abiding by implicit deals about what can and cannot be spoken about in order to maintain social cohesion and having the cultural competencies to know "where to step"; especially important in the context of anti-free speech regulations.

Conclusion

In some respects, there are positive signs regarding multiculturalism and youth in Malaysia, as illustrated by our small study showing young people's critical insight into racialized segregation, inequality and engagement across difference during the Najib era of "1Malaysia". This is supported by other research of this time, for example, Noor and Leong (2013, 720) cite Merdeka survey findings that the "younger generation living in urban areas are more likely to report having friends with other races" made through school and work. This everyday relationship-building is apparent to some extent in our research, although there are limits. Interpersonal relations across difference come up against structural inequality that is institutionalized through ethnic preferencing and entrenched through spatial and other kinds of segregation and routine everyday racism that is rarely formally acknowledged. As scholars have noted (Khoo 2014; Gabriel 2015), and as echoed by our participants, until ethnic inequality is more adequately recognized and addressed, deep and productive everyday mix cannot be possible, and everyday encounters frequently take the form of everyday racism. However, with the 2018 election of the Mahathir-led Pakatan Harapan government, which has ridden a wave of grassroots post-racial political momentum, it is timely and interesting to speculate on the real possibility of the dismantling of racial institutions and structures, including changes in education systems and other policies, that might yet address these structural inequalities.

It is also possible to foresee that an alternative national narrative, unmarked by multiracialism, might also be promoted, for example, a revised form of Mahathir's earlier and more inclusive "Bangsa Malaysia" (or "Malaysian race") policy that allows for a more critical engagement with race and difference (Gabriel 2011). Such an imaginary is sorely needed, as these Najib-era youth show. For our participants, integration and mix still predominantly occur through a paradigm of multiracialism, which produces and demands fixed and singular racial identity categories. Indeed, a benefit of the everyday multiculturalism framework is that it reveals the processes by which these racial categories are brought to life and operationalized in everyday encounters. While the young people in our research demonstrate considerable competencies and reflexivity in the pragmatic and strategic presentation of their racial identities, it is difficult for them to express hybridity and multiplicity and imagine more diverse and inclusive forms of Malaysianness.

This question of shifting national imaginaries also relates to that of the relationship between everyday convivialities and more formal politics of cosmopolitanism. Since this research was undertaken, Malaysia has experienced unprecedented trans-ethnic activism (by the Bersih movement amongst others), leading to the ousting of the Barisan Nasional coalition. Khoo (2014, 794) argues that cosmopolitanism has long been a civil society strategy to undo racialization in Malaysia, and cites the examples of progressive political movements and independent media makers forging trans-ethnic solidarities. This recent political transformation demonstrates the potential in such efforts that empower Malaysians to work towards a common goal in the face of longstanding race politics and the state discourse of racialization. There are now real possibilities for post-racial multiculturalism fostered by civic empowerment, trans-ethnic political solidarities and new kinds of activism. Significantly, youth are at the forefront of these political activities and cultural change, especially the young, urban, English-educated, multiethnic and cosmopolitan middle class (Gabriel 2015; see also Koh 2015), who played a leadership role in Bersih.

It is also important to reflect on how the everyday practices of less politicized young people connect with more organized or collective forms of alternative post-racial politics. We suggest that an everyday multiculturalism approach is important in identifying a critical micro-level of negotiation and contestation of the hegemony of the pluralist paradigm of race categorization in Malaysia that may cultivate critical dispositions and political solidarities. Attention to these processes can capture the "little publics" where young people's everyday multiculturalism occurs, and the intimate and mundane practices through which their cosmopolitan identities and solidarities can be forged and fostered.

Finally, we have shown how some connections amongst youth require the capacity to engage in forms of "modern" consumption, and especially the economic means to participate in global youth culture. In this respect, being a young "transcultural Malaysian" (Joseph 2014) cannot be disentangled from being an active member of global "modern" consumer culture. For young Malaysians, education, employment and intra-ethnic income disparity are more important than interethnic differences or defending Malay rights (Noor and Leong 2013, 720), and it is this holistic perspective, that engages questions of class and mobility as well as ethnicity, that needs to ground and perhaps animate our approaches to youth negotiations of belonging, identity and diversity. Young people are at new intersections of youth cultural, national and global belongings, new transitions to uncertain adulthoods and a global economy, not just ethnic politics as an isolated phenomenon, and these interrelated dimensions of their lives must be accounted for when we think about post-pluralist futures for Malaysian youth.

Disclosure statement

No potential conflict of interest was reported by the authors.

References

1Malaysia. 2018. *The Story of 1Malaysia*. Accessed March 19, 2018. http://www.1malaysia.com.my.

Ahmad, F., A. Salman, S. A. Rahim, L. Pantaweh, and A. L. Ahmad. 2013. "Interethnic Tolerance among Multiethnic Youth." *Journal of Asian Pacific Communication* 23 (2): 275–290.

Amin, A. 2002. "Ethnicity and the Multicultural City: Living with Diversity." *Environment and Planning A* 34: 959–980.

Ang, I. 2010. "Between Nationalism and Transnationalism: Multiculturalism in a Globalising World." *Centre for Cultural Research Occasional Paper Series* 1 (1): 1–14.

Aziz, N. A., N. A. Ismail, and M. Y. Yazid. 2013. "Stimulating the Spirit of Neighbourliness among Ethnicities in Residential Areas through Urban Cultural Landscapes." *Scottish Journal of Arts, Social Sciences and Scientific Studies* 2 (2): 41–52.

Daniels, T. P. 2010. "Urban Space, Belonging, and Inequality in Multi- Ethnic Housing Estates of Melaka, Malaysia." *Identities* 17: 2–3. 176–203.

Department of Statistics Malaysia. 2017. *Current Population Estimates 2016–2017.* https://www.dosm.gov.my/v1/index.php?r = column/cthemeByCat&cat = 155&bul_id = a1d1UTFZazd5ajJiRWFHNDduOXFFQT09&menu_id = L0pheU43NWJwRWVSZkIWdzQ4TlhUUT09.

Ferrarese, M. 2014. "Kami Semua Headbangers: Heavy Metal as Multiethnic Community Builder in Penang Island, Malaysia." *International Journal of Community Music* 7 (2): 153–171.

Gabriel, S. P. 2011. "Translating Bangsa Malaysia: Toward a New Cultural Politics of Malaysianness." *Critical Asian Studies* 43 (3): 349–372.

Gabriel, S. P. 2015. "The Meaning of Race in Malaysia: Colonial, Post-Colonial and Possible New Conjunctures." *Ethnicities* 15 (6): 782–809.

Harris, A. 2004. *Future Girl: Young Women in the 21st Century.* New York: Routledge.

Harris, A. 2013. *Young People and Everyday Multiculturalism.* New York: Routledge.

Jones, H., S. Neal, G. Mohan, K. Connell, A. Cochrane, and K. Bennett. 2015. "Urban Multiculture and Everyday Encounters in Semi-Public, Franchised Café Spaces." *The Sociological Review* 63: 644–661.

Joseph, C. 2014. *Growing up Female in Multi-ethnic Malaysia.* New York: Routledge.

Khoo, G. C. 2009. "Kopitiam: Discursive Cosmopolitan Spaces and National Identity in Malaysian Culture and Media." In *Everyday Multiculturalism*, edited by A. Wise and S. Velayutham, 87–104. Basingstoke: Palgrave Macmillan.

Khoo, G. C. 2014. "Introduction: Theorizing Different Forms of Belonging in a Cosmopolitan Malaysia." *Citizenship Studies* 18 (8): 791–806.

Koh, S. Y. 2015. "State-led Talent Return Migration Programme and the Doubly Neglected 'Malaysian Diaspora'." *Singapore Journal of Tropical Geography* 36 (2): 183–200.

Koh, S. Y. 2017. *Race, Education and Citizenship: Mobile Malaysians, British Colonial Legacies, and a Culture of Migration.* New York: Palgrave Macmillan.

Lim, J. 2013. "East Asian Trends in Malaysia: Negotiating Youth Identities, Culture and Citizenship via Social Media." *Situations* 7 (1): 21–42.

Nayak, A. 2003. *Race, Place and Globalization: Youth Cultures in a Changing World.* Oxford: Berg.

Noor, N. M., and C.-H. Leong. 2013. "Multiculturalism in Malaysia and Singapore: Contesting Models." *International Journal of Intercultural Relations* 37: 714–726.

Ooi, Sim Koay. 2015. "Understanding 1Malaysia: Analysis of Youth Perspectives." https://ssrn.com/abstract = 2697893 or http://dx.doi.org/10.2139/ssrn.2697893.

Salleh, S. M. 2013. "Unity in Diversity: Inculcating the Concept of 1Malaysia through Local Television Programmes." *Journal of Asian Pacific Communication* 23 (2): 183–195.

Semi, G., E. Colombo, I. Camozzi, and A. Frisina. 2009. "Practices of Difference: Analysing Multiculturalism in Everyday Life." In *Everyday Multiculturalism*, edited by A. Wise, and S. Velayutham. Basingstoke: Palgrave Macmillan.

Tamam, E. 2013. "Interracial Bridging Social Capital among Students of a Multicultural University in Malaysia." *Journal of College Student Development* 54 (1): 85–97.

Tamam, E., and S. E. Krauss. 2017. "Ethnic-related Diversity Engagement Differences in Intercultural Sensitivity among Malaysian Undergraduate Students." *International Journal of Adolescence and Youth* 22 (2): 137–150.

Thomas, M., and M. Butcher. 2003. *Ingenious: Emerging Youth Cultures in Urban Australia*. North Melbourne: Pluto Press.

Wise, A. 2009. "Everyday Multiculturalism: Transversal Crossings and Working Class Cosmopolitanisms." In *Everyday Multiculturalism*, edited by A. Wise, and S. Velayutham. Basingstoke: Palgrave Macmillan.

Wise, A., and G. Noble. 2016. "Convivialities: An Orientation." *Journal of Intercultural Studies* 37 (5): 423–431.

Wise, A., and S. Velayutham. 2009. "Introduction: Multiculturalism and Everyday Life." In *Everyday Multiculturalism*, edited by A. Wise, and S. Velayutham. Basingstoke: Palgrave Macmillan.

The limits of "multiculturalism without diversity": multi-ethnic students and the negotiation of "difference" in South Korean schools

Jessica Walton 🆔

ABSTRACT

Since 2006, although South Korean "multiculturalism" policies have attempted to grapple with increasing ethnic and cultural diversity within Korean society, a homogenous national imaginary continues to inform these policies. I refer to the government's approach to multiculturalism as "multiculturalism without diversity" to describe the limits of a multiculturalism anchored within an ethnic nationalistic framing of "difference". Based on findings from an ethnographic study in South Korean primary schools, this paper examines how tensions between the reality of increasing diversity and a multicultural policy approach that maintains homogenous representations of Korean identity played out among Grade 5/6 children from Korean mono-ethnic and multi-ethnic backgrounds. Although there were limits to the ways children could assert authority, this paper analyses the mundane everyday practices and strategies that multi-ethnic children used to attempt to reassert and reinsert themselves at school and more broadly, within the possibility of a more critical Korean multiculturalism.

Introduction

South Korea (hereafter Korea) is a country that has experienced rapid increases in immigration since the 1990s and as of 2015, when I conducted this research, the number of foreign-born residents or citizens living in Korea exceeded 1.4 million or about 2.7% of the population, which is a 141% increase since 2007 (KOSIS 2015). This increase in migration since the 1990s is attributed mainly to migrant workers and female marriage migrants from countries such as China, Japan, Vietnam and the Philippines (KESS 2014; Kim 2011). These changing demographics began to challenge the limits of a Korean national identity founded on racial-ethnic homogeneity (Shin, Freda, and Yi 1999; Shin 2006) and in response since 2006, the government selectively developed policies to support the social integration of marriage migrants and their children and multicultural support plans were implemented, resulting in the establishment of multicultural family support centres and Korean language and cultural classes (Kim 2011). As the number of children of so-called "multicultural families" (i.e. *damunhwa kajeong*, constituting at least one person who is an immigrant by marriage or who acquired Korean nationality through naturalization) (Kim 2007, 2011, 2012; MOGEF 2008) began to attend school, schools also became sites targeted by multiculturalism education policies (Grant and Ham 2013).

Coinciding with the development of multiculturalism policies in the last decade, there has been a surge in discourse about "multiculturalism" within Korean society in the media (e.g. Ahn 2012; Hundt, Walton, and Lee 2019) and in academia (e.g. Kim 2011, 2012; Lie 2015; Watson 2012). Although these discussions are considered a significant shift and critical step toward developing a more inclusive approach to diversity (Lim 2010), current policies only recognize cultural diversity to the extent that the government can assimilate those cultural differences (while ignoring racial differences that remain visible markers of difference) (Choi 2010; J. K. Kim 2011; Lee 2017). Policies have also been critiqued for their selective focus rather than considering the role of all Koreans and Korean society as a whole (Kim 2011; Watson 2012).

Despite increasing scholarly attention to multiculturalism in Korea, with the exception of a few studies (e.g. Kim and Kim 2012; Lee 2017; Paik 2010), there is less attention paid to the children of "multicultural families", who have become the main target of multiculturalism policy, especially within the education sector. Research has mainly focused on critiques of multiculturalism policy rather than an "everyday multiculturalism", which examines how institutional structures affect how diversity is relationally enacted through mundane practices in familiar spaces like markets, schools and neighbourhoods (Harris 2009; Ho 2011; Wise and Velayutham 2009). There is a lack of deep understanding about how tensions between multiculturalism policy and everyday experiences of multiculturalism play out in everyday spaces in terms of how racial, ethnic and cultural homogeneity is both reinforced and refuted as well as the diversity of people's experiences classified as constituting those of "multicultural families". Although it is not within the scope of this paper for a full discussion of multiculturalism education policy, the point this paper seeks to make is that there is a gap between the focus of Korea's multiculturalism education policy which centres on language and cultural knowledge acquisition and multi-ethnic children's experiences of racial difference and racism in everyday life. The conflation of culture and race and a policy omission of a critical understanding of race fails to account for multi-ethnic children's everyday experiences of exclusion, despite cultural and linguistic fluency, based on a dual hierarchy of perceived racial differences and country of origin (Lee 2017). Harris (2014, 573) argues that when considering more theoretical issues about diversity and globalization, especially for young people, it is critical to examine how these issues are made locally meaningful by looking "closely at their strategies for belonging and engagement in their communities".

In order to consider how tensions between growing ethnic diversity and the (re)production of imagined ethnic-national homogeneity through "multiculturalism" policies are playing out in everyday life, this paper examines these dynamics through the peer relations and mundane everyday practices of primary school children from mono-ethnic and multi-ethnic Korean backgrounds in school spaces. Due to the stigma associated with terminology used in multiculturalism policies such as "multicultural family students" and because the students in my study all identified as culturally Korean, I use "multi-ethnic" to refer to students with at least one parent who is not ethnically Korean and "mono-ethnic" to refer to students from families with ethnically Korean parents. A key question that this paper seeks to address is: how do multi-ethnic Korean children create spaces in which to confront underlying exclusionary practices among mono-ethnic Korean peers at school and assert themselves in ways that might negotiate and challenge an "othering" ethno-nationalistic form of multiculturalism?

To explore this question, my theoretical and conceptual framework draws on everyday multiculturalism (Wise and Velayutham 2009), which refers to not only how questions of race, ethnicity and culture are negotiated in everyday situations but also how those local specificities are connected to broader structural regimes (i.e. reflected in policy approaches to multiculturalism), which affect how the local is understood. In analysing the students' interactions, I draw connections between the state-based racism reinforced through multiculturalism education policy founded on hierarchies of belonging according to race, class and country of origin (Lee 2017) and the experiences of multi-ethnic students, which include experiences of everyday racism (Essed 1991), as they navigate these hierarchies at school. Drawing on theories of complexity (Watkins 2011), alterity (Noble 2011), and hierarchies of belonging, racism and everyday otherness (Essed 1991; Kim 2011; Lee 2017; Radford 2016), I argue that it is in everyday interactions that these tensions are most felt and by analysing children's peer relations at school and the strategies that multi-ethnic students use to navigate intra-ethnic and inter-ethnic differences, we can understand how their experiences speak to or speak against the aims of a top-down governmental multiculturalism.

Methodology

In 2015, I conducted ethnographic school-based observations (for 3 months, which is part of a longer research program that I have undertaken in Korea since 2007) and semi-structured interviews with Grade 5/6 students at three government primary schools in South Korea (Gyeonggi province) – Baram School (Yongin – in a middle to upper middle-class area), Namu School (Yongin – in a low to middle-class area) and Hosu School (Pyeongtaek – in a working-class area near a U.S. army base). I chose Gyeonggi province because this province has the highest number of multi-ethnic primary school students with about 15.7 multi-ethnic students per school (Korean Educational Statistical Service (KESS) 2014). However, other provinces such as Jeollanam province have a higher proportion of multi-ethnic students compared to the total student population at 5.6% whereas Gyeonggi province is 2.7% (KESS 2014). The schools who were invited to participate were contacted through a Korean teacher at Baram School who had previously been to Australia on a teacher exchange program and who was recommended to me. Because I used convenience sampling, my participant group was limited to the demographic background of the students at these three schools. However, the participants in this research are not intended to be a representative sample. In terms of the number of multi-ethnic students at the participating schools, I was told that there was no formal systematic process that the schools used to proactively identify multi-ethnic students. Therefore, the figures in Table 1 are estimates from the schools based on those families who voluntarily identified themselves as "multicultural families" or those the teachers identified as multi-ethnic based on proxies such as the students' physical features such as skin colour, eye shape and hair colour or if the mother or father had a non-Korean name when they enrolled their child at the school. Additionally, students who have a mother or father who is not Korean may not be identified as "multicultural" because most students are given a Korean name and take the father's Korean family name and some students do not look any different to the other students. For example, there were no students with Korean Chinese parents identified in Grade 5 and 6 in the classes that participated in my research but it is possible that there were students who were overlooked by teachers. There were two groups of participants, children who had one non-Korean parent ($n = 7$) (see Table 2) and children with two Korean parents ($n = 13$). All of the children except one were born in Korea and all could speak Korean fluently. Ethics approval was received from my University and I use pseudonyms for all participants and the schools involved.

Table 1. Multi-ethnic student demographics at the research schools.

School	Total students	Total multi-ethnic students	% of multi-ethnic students
Namu	727	8	1.1%
Baram	807	10	1.2%
Hosu	833	33	4.0%

Table 2. Multi-ethnic students who participated.

Namu School	Baram School	Hosu School
Jeong-hwan (Filipina mother, Korean father)	Tae-heon (German father, Korean mother)	Min-jae (Russian mother, Korean father)
Yeon-seo (Thai mother, Korean father)	Ye-jun (Japanese mother, Korean father)	Joo-won (Nepalese mother, Korean father)
		Ha-eun (Japanese mother, Korean father)

My approach for the classroom-based observations was to sit with the students at a desk or on a chair in the back of the classroom. During class, my interactions with students were limited by the structured lessons and the teacher's presence. It was mainly during the class breaks that the students and I could interact freely. For the interviews, I used a semi-structured schedule with questions about students' interests, hobbies, things they like or do not like, worries and dreams, friends and family and experiences of ethnic and cultural diversity. I also used friendship circles (Smith 2005) to capture their perspectives on who their closest friends were and people who were just friends or acquaintances. All interviews were conducted in Korean except for when students preferred to do the interview in English. Interviews were transcribed and the Korean interviews were then translated into English. To analyse the data, I read over the interviews and fieldnotes several times and conducted line-by-line coding using qualitative analytical software to capture themes arising from the data, which included questions of identity, strategies for belonging, friendship and intimate and peripheral encounters with difference.

A note on positionality

On my first day at each of the three schools, the students had a similar reaction to my claim that I was from Australia. Students glanced at me curiously and whispered to each other asking if I were really a *oegukin* (foreigner) and if I were really from Australia. When I introduced myself, my non-native Korean language ability surprised students and they wondered if I could speak English well because I looked Korean. My initial presence as questionably "different" affected some of my interactions with the students. I could speak Korean with them but even just the knowledge that I was "different" meant that some students avoided interacting with me.

My indeterminate position affected my ability to become closer to some students, which is the case in any research project that requires the researcher to navigate intersecting positionalities. However, my in-between status as "not quite adult/teacher" and "not quite student" and someone who was not familiar with the school and classroom procedures was also a strength. I was someone that the students could teach and help rather than someone perceived as having all the knowledge. Over time, most students warmed to me and I was even adopted into some of the girls' friendship groups. However, I was also still an adult and a researcher so I had to be careful to continuously reflect on my own behaviours to lessen the hierarchy between us but also to understand that their behaviours would also change according to my fluid position as "least-adult" (Froerer 2016, 96) or in my case, an adult but not quite adult who was also not a teacher. Additionally, because I am not a native Korean speaker, I could not always capture some of the conversational nuances among the students particularly slang terms. However, this also proved useful for asking them questions and learning from them. At the same time, speaking English as well as Korean allowed me to connect with some of the students who wanted to practice their English or multi-ethnic students like Min-jae and Tae-heon who shared a special connection by being able to use their multi-lingual abilities. Finally, I did not take on a disciplinary role and my behaviours mirrored the students such as sitting on the floor together or entering the back door rather than the front door of the classroom where the teacher and other adults entered and left.

The following sections examine the concept of everyday multiculturalism in relation to hierarchies of cultural belonging and everyday racism experienced by multi-ethnic students at school. I draw connections between the stigma of otherness reinforced in multicultural education policy and the multi-ethnic students' experiences as "cultural others". This is followed by an analysis of the strategies some of the multi-ethnic students used to navigate exclusionary practices. The paper aims to contribute to an understanding of "everyday multiculturalism" (Wise and Velayutham 2009) within schools in a Korean context, which challenges the "cultural othering" embedded in Korean multiculturalism policies.

Tensions of "difference" and experiences of racism within a "multiculturalism without diversity"

A key issue at the heart of Korean multiculturalism policies is that they do not challenge hierarchies of belonging founded on race, class and country of origin (Lee 2017) which is reinforced through the terminology used to designate "multicultural families" and "multicultural family students/children" as "Other" (Grant and Ham 2013; Kang 2010), thus contributing to a dual "cultural hierarchy between Koreans and non-Koreans" (Kim 2011, 1583). In Korea, discriminatory attitudes toward people from different countries are affected by intersections of place, race and class (Lee 2017). For example, people from Southeast Asia are perceived to be from countries that are poor, thus not modern, and "undesirable" compared to white people from Western European and North American countries considered to be modern and wealthy and therefore "desirable". Furthermore, people whose physical differences signal a multi-racial background experience additional stigma due to the social weight placed on patrilineal bloodlines (Lim 2010). Now with a declining birth-rate and an aging population, the Korean government has actively sought to support "multicultural families" with a specific focus on mainly Korean men (rather than foreign men), a foreign wife and their children, thus maintaining the patrilineal bloodline.

A patriarchal ethnic nationalism continues to remain a core problem within these policies because they do not explicitly "confront the strategies by which homogeneous identities are constructed and maintained" (Shin, Freda, and Yi 1999, 474) and also reinforce gendered inequalities (Lee 2008). By maintaining a core Korean culture and selectively grouping particular "cultural others" under the label *damunhwa* (despite this term meaning literally, "many/multiple cultures"), multiculturalism policy in Korea appears to be at most a cultural assimilation policy predicated on socializing and integrating a particular group of people with migrant backgrounds to become more "like" other Koreans so they can fit into existing structures and productively contribute to Korean society without challenging an imagined Korean ethno-racial homogeneity. This produces a situation in which Korea has developed a policy of selective group assimilation for the purpose of nation-building while calling it "multiculturalism policy".

I argue that this contradiction creates a policy of "multiculturalism without diversity", which is to say it creates the illusion of supporting multiculturalism as a policy in name only, while in practice, continues to view cultural difference as an impediment to social inclusion. By appropriating the term "multiculturalism" and using it to only refer to a select subset of the Korean population, Korean multiculturalism is a form of a Korea-centred nation-building that prioritizes a "core" Korean identity. By focusing on "multicultural families" in multiculturalism policy, the government seeks to address nation-centred issues, namely Korea's low birth rate and an aging population. As a consequence, Korea's increasing racial, ethnic and cultural diversity becomes less about implications for how Korean society is changing as a whole (not only special policies for particular migrants) and more about the existence of cultural diversity that needs to be realigned according to an overarching and dominant Korean identity represented as culturally homogenous rather than diverse that can ultimately suit the economic needs of the nation.

In the context of education, although there has been a gradual shift from "mono-ethnicism ... [to] notions of cultural diversity and multiculturalism", in curriculum documents and policy statements, nation-centered content remains dominant in multicultural education (Moon 2010, 5). In an analysis of multiculturalism education policies and subsequent revisions from 2006 to 2012, Grant and Ham (2013, 84) found that recent policies such as the 2012 policy "does not seek to understand students' diversity or to change the privilege and power of the dominant culture", thus re-stigmatizing students who are classified as "multicultural family students". Instead multiculturalism education policies selectively target a subset of the population considered not Korean enough and then take an assimilationist top-down approach by focusing on language and culture while ignoring exclusionary practices based on race and country of origin (Hong 2010). This largely ignores diversity within categories such as "multicultural family students" and overlooks how these students perceive their own sense of identity and belonging (Walton 2018) as well as the everyday ways in which students are navigating the changing ethno-racial landscape, particularly at key sites such as schools.

For multi-ethnic children, their Korean background connects them to Korea and yet their difference reflected by one of their parent's non-Korean background puts this Korean background in tension with an imagined homogenous identity. As Noble (2011, 832) argues:

> ... while we experience alterity in a seemingly contingent fashion – we "bump" into it – it is nevertheless the result of complex processes of migration, economic development, urbanization and policies for managing diversity which show how much the market and government are not removed from "forms of life" but give shape to its textures.

For children, schools are places of forced togetherness where they study and play alongside people they would not necessarily meet outside of school. Because of their more pronounced "otherness", multi-ethnic students such as Joo-won, who were perceived to be more "different" (darker skin colour, parent's country of origin) than other multi-ethnic students, had more difficulty entering the inner circles of other children's friendship groups. Toward the end of my time at Hosu school, I told the Korean English teacher that I had just finished an interview with Joo-Won. She said that she heard Joo-Won does not have friends and he had some trouble the year before when he allegedly hit, kicked or punched a few other students. She did not know if the same thing was happening the year I was there but she did say she heard he struggles in class and does not participate. Despite this knowledge, she said that as a teacher, she does not notice the multi-ethnic students' "differences" (therefore, taking a colour-blind approach), but she said other students do see that difference, especially when it comes to skin colour and she thinks they can "feel the difference" so they do not try to be friends with him (Walton, forthcoming). Whereas the teachers concentrated on any cultural differences rather than racial differences, particularly Korean language difficulties that might affect multi-ethnic students' learning, which is reflective of the focus of multiculturalism education policy and its omission of a discussion of race and racism, the mono-ethnic students focused on the multi-ethnic students' racial and perceived class difference based on the multi-ethnic students' skin colour and their parents' country of origin (Lee 2017). Joo-Won and Jeong-hwan experienced first-hand a cultural hierarchy of belonging (Kim 2011; Lee 2017) due to the underlying racism and classed stigma that structured their interactions. On an everyday basis, other students would just walk away when they approached them or tried to play with them.

This feeling of otherness could be described as "everyday otherness", which according to Radford (2016, 8132), "takes place in everyday encounters between members of diverse communities ... [and] is reflective of a lack of understanding and/or ignorance about one another. It also reflects a lack of personal relationship and engagement with 'the other'". Although there was certainly a lack of understanding and a lack of a personal relationship with multi-ethnic students like Joo-won, mono-ethnic students were still actively engaging with Joo-won even if it did not take on recognizable forms of engagement (e.g. speaking directly to each other). The other students interacted with Joo-won by negotiating the space between themselves and Joo-won, which took the form of consistently ignoring him and maintaining distance from him. These negotiations of "otherness" among the students were occurring within a broader social context in which multiculturalism policy constructs "difference" as something to be assimilated through Korean cultural and linguistic knowledge and skill acquisition. However, the multi-ethnic students who took part in my study could speak Korean fluently and had lived the majority of their lives, if not all their lives, in Korea. Their continued experiences of "difference", despite no linguistic or cultural barriers, meant that their racialised differences impacted on their belonging not only at school but within a larger conversation about what it means to be Korean (Paik 2010).

Within this context of racialised hierarchies and situated within a regulated institutional school context, the extent to which students, and in particular multi-ethnic students, could assert themselves was limited. However, multi-ethnic students also used strategies to create space for themselves that resisted the "othering" effects of a "multiculturalism" that only recognized their difference in an attempt to subsume those differences. These strategies included: (1) strategic invisibility; and (2) skilful resistance.

Strategic invisibility

For students who could be seen as unproblematically Korean, and often were by both students and teachers, there was the option of choosing not to reveal their multi-ethnic background. On the one hand, this might be seen as a coping mechanism, which was how teachers talked about it, saying they understood why these students did not want other students to know. Their decision not to draw attention to themselves in this way was rationalized as something that stemmed from individual sensitivity or lack of confidence.

However, from the multi-ethnic students' perspectives, this decision was also something that could be described as "strategic invisibility" or strategies used to avoid disclosing one's ethnic or cultural differences when those differences are potentially stigmatized within social hierarchies of difference. Firstly, because of the exclusion that multi-ethnic students with darker skin experienced, those who could pass as only being Korean, such as Ha-Eun and Yeon-Seo had a vested interest in keeping their difference invisible. For example, during the interview, Ha-Eun compared herself to Joo-Won who was in the same class as her and explained why she does not want all the students to know that her mother is Japanese. She said, "If it doesn't show that you are from a different culture like me it is okay, but if it shows like Joo-won, those kids get bullied a lot and have a difficult time becoming friends with others" (Walton 2018, 104). She also said that some mono-ethnic students know such as her friend, Min-a but she does not talk openly about her Japanese background in class because not all the students know. When I interviewed Min-a, she said that she is interested in Japanese anime but said she does not talk about Japanese culture with Ha-eun and instead she said, "A male classmate likes Japan so I talk about it with him" (Walton 2018, 103). The guardedness that Ha-eun exhibited and which was protected by friends such as Min-a, describes a "strategic invisibility" that could be a way to seek "comfort", which Noble (2005, 114) describes as "the 'fit' we experience in relation to the spaces we inhabit and the practices we perform". By downplaying the possibility for perceived difference through strategic invisibility, Ha-eun sought to find a way to feel "comfort" among her peers. She was able to do this by refraining from talking about her Japanese background and also because she was not visibly different from her mono-ethnic peers.

Yeon-seo also found "comfort" in being "invisible" and said she likes coming to school because she can play with her friends. In the interview, she mentioned about five friends whereas Joo-won only mentioned one person who is enrolled at a different school and one person who was in a different homeroom class at his school but who was only a peripheral friend. In a moment of profound loneliness, Jeong-hwan explained to me during the interview that he could not do the friendship circle exercise because he did not have any friends. Given the power dynamics among children within the classroom space, Ha-eun felt that it was better for her to minimize her Japanese background and was in a privileged position to do so compared to Jeong-hwan. Children such as Ha-eun and Yeon-seo were performing a strategic invisibility within the pressures of school spaces where they could not choose who was in their class and so had to devise their own strategies for "getting along". For these children, the ambiguous lines between being seen as "different" or "not different" required ongoing regulation, which did not always sit "comfortably" with them but served the purpose of creating some resemblance of "comfort" at school. As Ha-eun told me, she would like others to know about her Japanese mother because she is proud of her but she cannot be completely free with this aspect of herself among her classmates.

Secondly, the students' strategic invisibility can be seen as a way to reject a "multiculturalism" policy that uses an "othering" approach to ethnic differences by separating them as people who are not quite Korean and who need to be made Korean. They reject the stigma embedded in multiculturalism education policy that positions multi-ethnic students and their families as separate from other Korean students and families such as providing after-school classes rather than embedding multiculturalism education within the national curriculum. They also reject the assumption that they are somehow "less Korean" than other mono-ethnic Korean students. For these students, including students such as Joo-won who experienced more overt racism and discrimination, they said that they feel Korean (Walton 2018). Yeon-seo was the only student who said she felt "half–half because of my mother". When I asked her if she had been to any multicultural events, she said she went to one with her mother but she decided to wear a Korean hanbok rather than Thai traditional dress. Min-jae, a Grade 5 student at Hosu School with a Russian mother and Korean father, said during an interview that he visited Russia for one month but he felt he "cannot even stay there half a month". He said compared to Korea, in Russia he could "get close friends and that was fun" whereas in Korea he said his closest friend is his cat. However, he said he missed Korea and his father and then explained, "I feel I'm really Korean ... because I was born in here, in this place, in this ground and like one of my parents is Korean, like my father" (Walton 2018, 109). However, at school his Russian mother is the point of difference the students focus on. Mono-ethnic students frequently told me, "His mother is Russian!" While statements about feeling Korean may be perceived as successful assimilation and a positive outcome of the government's "multiculturalism" policy to "include" children like Min-jae so they feel like they "belong", Min-jae's clear lack of belonging at school and lack of friends shows that this is not the case. On the one hand, Min-jae's reasons for why he feels Korean reaffirm the majority of ethno-nationalistic and gendered criteria for determining one's "Koreanness" (e.g. patrilineal claims to belonging, linguistic and cultural capabilities, being born in Korea). However, Min-jae's declaration and his multiracial background also challenge the very basis on which Korean ethnicnationalism is defined by questioning the isomorphism of race and culture (Gupta and Ferguson 1992) as well as ethnicity and nationality (Shin, Freda, and Yi 1999). At the same time, deploying strategic invisibility can also serve to maintain a racial hierarchy by not unsettling underlying assumptions about race. This strategy was only possible for students who could "pass" as having two Korean parents.

Skilful resistance

Another way multi-ethnic students tried to work against discrimination and feelings of "otherness" was through what could be called, "skilful resistance". This involved drawing on skills that may still set them apart from others but were used in spite of how other students reacted to them. For example, Min-jae used his stronger English language skills to be able to talk with me about things other students were not interested in and he also acted as an occasional translator. This skill set him apart from other students as much as it drew them to him to take advantage of his ability to talk more easily with me. Furthermore, as Min-jae explained in the interview, he felt his first language was English rather than Korean or Russian because he spent his earlier years watching hours of YouTube. When I spoke with him in Korean, he would often reply in English or insist on us both speaking English. It took a few weeks before I realized that Min-jae spoke English because he kept to himself and most other kids did not interact with him. However, as time passed, he began to talk with me and other students started hanging around him a little more because they had not realized he could speak English fairly well. Min-jae enjoyed having someone who he could talk with about his eclectic interests and did not seem to care about the other students' reactions to him. Tae-heon also used his English skills to have an advantage over other students. He was proud of being from Germany and his dream was to be a soccer player and play for Germany, not Korea. On my last day, he wrote me a letter in German and said I could use Google Translate to read it. He had carefully folded up the letter and told me he did not want other students to see and I could read it later. When I told some of the teachers about both Min-jae and Tae-heon's language skills, they were surprised. During a field trip, Tae-heon's homeroom teacher called Tae-heon over to confirm what I had told them about his ability to speak English and German. As Tae-heon stood awkwardly at the edge of the teachers' picnic mat, the teacher continued asking him questions, including if his mother is Korean and as proof, asked for his mother's name. After Tae-heon left to play with the other students, the teacher told me it is odd that he has his mother's last name instead of his German father's. All of the multi-ethnic students had been given Korean forenames and all of them except Tae-heon had ethnic Korean fathers, which meant they also had Korean surnames thus reflecting the patrilineal Korean family lineage. In Tae-heon's case, he had been given his Korean mother's family name so that he would fit in. One of the other teachers said he also has a German first name, but this name is never used at school. As for Min-jae, he was often scolded in English class for not doing his homework or for not doing the work during class, which gave his teacher the impression that his English is not strong. However, Min-jae told me that he finds the English classes boring because he already knows a lot of what is being taught in the textbook.

As Watkins (2011, 849) argues "within education and in dealing with other realms of the social, it is the complexities of the practices of individual actors that can provide useful insights into the system of which they are a part". From the teachers' perspective, the students could speak Korean fluently just like the mono-ethnic Korean students and so in practice, they taught the students in the same way. This may be seen as inclusive, however, it also reduced the complexity of the students in a way that did not consider a more expansive understanding of their lived experiences, including abilities such as speaking English or German. Although Min-jae and Tae-heon could momentarily create space for themselves that resisted not only the reduction of complexity but also the way in which their complexity was reduced, it was also a contested and fleeting space. This was demonstrated by Tae-heon's teacher's questioning, which served to further position Tae-heon as "other" by questioning the validity of his Korean name after asking about his English and German language skills. During this interaction between Tae-heon and his teacher, Tae-heon's complex sense of identity was reduced to a set of different culturally fetishized parts, a common occurrence in Korea's approach to cultural diversity (Kim 2011), and laid out as if they were simply disparate aspects of someone's identity that could be probed and examined. Rather than understanding "how people 'inhabit' such complexity as a lived reality" (Noble 2011, 833), the complexity of Tae-heon's identity as his lived reality was reduced to ethnicised parts to "confirm" his incomplete belonging as someone from a multi-ethnic background. Tae-heon's skilful resistance by asserting the complexities of his identity through language was subjugated by his teacher's "othering" approach.

At Namu School, Jeong-hwan used a different form of skilful resistance. His teacher observed that compared to last year, she could tell he was participating more in class and trying harder at his studies. She said that last year he did not participate much and was often bullied. His sister was in Grade 6 at the time and she was also bullied partly due to her lack of personal hygiene. Their mother had divorced and left to go back to the Philippines and so their Korean grandmother cared for them. The reason for their experiences of bullying was considered to be more of an individualized case of personal hygiene but, with a mother from the Philippines, was primarily grounded in a dual hierarchical racial framework that codes country of origin and colour according to a scale of favourability and acceptance (Lee 2017). Jeong-hwan was also facing this dual hierarchy in the other students' responses to him. The mono-ethnic students did not speak to Jeong-hwan except to tell him to "go away" but the majority of the time, they responded to him through their body language – by turning their bodies away from him, frowning at his efforts and completely ignoring his presence. Their responses served to reinforce a racialised hierarchy of exclusion. During gym class and during class breaks, he often moved around, moving his body in exaggerated ways to fill the space between himself and the other students. During one gym class, the other students were running around so he also bounced around jumping and smiling despite the other students giving him sideways glances and physically moving their bodies away from him. There were many times when Jeong-hwan imitated the other students, running around when other boys were running around, inserting himself into other students' games, participating in class even when he forgot a textbook or his recorder for music class. Even though each time his encounters with other students were extremely short-lived because other students told him off for trying to play with them or by moving away from him and ignoring him, Jeong-hwan kept trying. During English class when most of the students were copying the answers from the back of the book, Jeong-hwan continued trying to answer the questions on his own even when other students pointed out he could just look at the answer key. Each time the students rejected him, it was heartbreaking to watch and when we did the interview together, Jeong-hwan said he could not do the "friendship circle" exercise because he did not have any friends. Despite this, Jeong-hwan continued to try to narrow the lack of closeness between himself and the other students by taking up space both by answering questions in class and physically moving around the classroom rather than just sitting at his desk during breaks like I saw other multi-ethnic students do, such as Joo-won.

Overall, skilful resistance was not just about developing an individualized or inward skill such as resilience or self-confidence, as with Jeong-hwan, or using language skills, as was the case with Min-jae and Tae-heon. Rather, their skills and confidence were used strategically within an uneven playing field to attempt to skilfully negotiate the "everyday otherness" (Radford 2016) within the classroom space and to reinsert themselves in a way that resisted their peers' exclusion. The multi-ethnic students negotiated their "alterity" within a "schema of perception" filtered through a multiculturalism education policy that positions these students and their families as separate and different from mono-ethnic Korean students and their families. As Noble (2011, 838) writes:

> Schemas of perception shape policy and programs as much as they do mundane practice … they shape multicultural policy at a much broader level as well: the ways that the state configures the 'clients' of multiculturalism, those whose needs are to be 'serviced' and 'tolerated', and those who do the tolerating.

Although the multi-ethnic students' efforts were not always successful given how marginalized they were in a mostly ethnically homogenous school environment, their efforts were significant in that they were not simply passive but were active subjects who were attempting to re-frame the way their alterity was perceived among their peers. This also challenges the one-dimensional way in which they are also represented in multiculturalism education policy as passive recipients requiring linguistic and cultural resources to be assimilated. The multi-ethnic students in my study did not require these resources and instead, their experiences point to the need to critically address racialised and classed hierarchies of belonging embedded in Korean society which cannot simply be addressed through a "multiculturalism without diversity" focused more on assimilation of a subset of the Korean population rather than taking a whole-of-society transformative approach (Banks 1996; Grant and Ham 2013).

Conclusion

In Korea, schools are targeted by government multicultural education policies that provide support for students, such as Korean as a second language classes and financial subsidies, but also ultimately aim to instil a strong Korean identity that will serve the purposes of the nation-state. Due to a focus on ethnic and cultural difference that only recognizes difference in order to minimize it, these differences become stigmatized (associated with poor, uneducated, unclean). Furthermore, a deliberate lack of attention to race, by focusing on cultural differences, fails to account for the racialised hierarchies that form the basis of Korea's ethnic nationalism that merges race, ethnicity and culture with national identity. By focusing on "culture" as somehow more inclusive and "non-hierarchical" (Lentin 2005), existing structural hierarchies of difference along lines of race, ethnicity, culture and country of origin persist (Lee 2017). Because of this limited and "othering" approach to diversity, Korea's "multiculturalism" policy is less about reimagining a Korean society that includes multiple kinds of belonging that are not necessarily commensurate with a top-down Korean national identity and instead, is more about reinforcing Korean ethno-nationalism. This creates a policy context in which diversity exists but is "othered" as "not Korean" and therefore is not allowed to fully exist. This approach to "multiculturalism without diversity" is excluding the very people who the Korean government is allegedly trying to "include" and who are instead, through this "inclusion", marginalized as "Other" in everyday spaces, such as schools, even though they identify as Korean (Walton 2018). As a result, this approach to diversity which is "othered" within an imagined homogenous society requires those who are considered to represent ethnic and cultural diversity, such as the multi-ethnic children in this study, to negotiate spaces where they can assert themselves, albeit in limited ways due to the racialised hierarchies that structure interactions at school.

In terms of the everyday multiculturalism at the schools, because the majority of students at the schools in my study were from mono-ethnic Korean backgrounds, racial, ethnic and cultural differences did not play a major role in their everyday lives and so "how cultural diversity is experienced and negotiated on the ground in everyday situations" (Wise and Velayutham 2009, 2) was not explicit. However, for multi-ethnic students, especially those with darker skin whose differences were seen as "too different", their everyday experiences of difference were a key factor that structured their lives at school, particularly among their peers. For these multi-ethnic students, their racialised ethnic and classed difference became a focal point for other mono-ethnic Korean students to avoid potential encounters with them, serving to actively exclude them from friendship groups. Therefore, a Korean everyday multiculturalism at school was more implicit meaning that students were still navigating "difference" and "bumping into alterity" (Noble 2011) but this was occurring within relatively rigid structures that resisted the complexity of the multi-ethnic students' experiences. This is partly due to the limited way multiculturalism education policies frame multi-ethnic students' alterity from the outset, which influenced how the schools in my study approached the students. Because the multi-ethnic students were culturally and linguistically fluent, the difficulties they faced along racialised and classed hierarchies of belonging were not fully addressed. At the same time, the multi-ethnic students' stigmatized perception by their peers, some more than others, meant that despite the multi-ethnic students identifying as Korean, most could not overcome the everyday otherness exhibited through experiences of everyday racism that was embedded in interactions with their peers. Multiculturalism education policies which aim to minimize difficulties multi-ethnic children and their families experience do so in a way that simultaneously attempt to assimilate cultural difference while stigmatizing that difference.

Rather than a form of "multiculturalism without diversity" that stigmatizes particular groups of people in order to "help them" become more "Korean", what is required is a critical examination that involves an understanding of Korean identity that is itself multiple and diverse rather than a minoritised "diversity" that exists outside of or alongside a homogenized Korean identity. Although not always successful given hierarchical power structures which limited their efforts, the multi-ethnic students' negotiation of "difference" through everyday practices of strategic invisibility or skilful resistance highlight ways their efforts unsettle a national imaginary that attempts to maintain an illusion of "multiculturalism without diversity". This allows space for a more critical understanding of diversity that challenges not only what it means to be "Korean" but also the basis on which the question is asked.

Acknowledgements

This research was funded by a Deakin University Central Research Grant for 2015 and writing was supported by an Australian Research Council Fellowship (DE160100922). I wish to thank the editors and anonymous reviewers for their engaged and constructive feedback during the review process.

Disclosure statement

No potential conflict of interest was reported by the author.

Funding

This research was funded by a Deakin University Central Research Grant for 2015 and writing was supported by an Australian Research Council Fellowship (DE160100922).

ORCID

Jessica Walton ⓘ http://orcid.org/0000-0003-3876-2994

References

Ahn, Ji-Hyun. 2012. "Transforming Korea Into a Multicultural Society: Reception of Multiculturalism Discourse and its Discursive Disposition in Korea." *Asian Ethnicity* 13 (1): 97–109.

Banks, James A. 1996. *Multicultural Education, Transformative Knowledge, and Action: Historical and Contemporary Perspectives*. New York: Teacher College Press.

Choi, Jungsoon. 2010. "Educating Citizens in a Multicultural Society: The Case of South Korea." *The Social Studies* 101: 174–178.

Essed, Philomena. 1991. *Understanding Everyday Racism: An Interdisciplinary Theory*. Newbury Park: Sage.

Froerer, Peggy. 2016. "Questions and Curiosities, Ignorance and Understanding: Ethnographic Encounters with Children in Central India." In *Children: Ethnographic Encounters*, edited by Catherine Allerton, 87–99. London: Bloomsbury.

Grant, Carl A., and Sejung Ham. 2013. "Multicultural Education Policy in South Korea: Current Struggles and Hopeful Vision." *Multicultural Education Review* 5 (1): 67–95.

Gupta, Akhil, and James Ferguson. 1992. "Beyond 'Culture': Space, Identity and the Politics of Difference." *Cultural Anthropology* 7: 6–23.

Harris, Anita. 2009. "Shifting the Boundaries of Cultural Spaces: Young People and Everyday Multiculturalism." *Social Identities: Journal for the Study of Race, Nation and Culture* 15 (2): 187–205.

Harris, Anita. 2014. "Conviviality, Conflict and Distanciation in Young People's Local Multicultures." *Journal of Intercultural Studies* 35 (6): 571–587.

Ho, Christina. 2011. "Respecting the Presence of Others: School Micropublics and Everyday Multiculturalism." *Journal of Intercultural Studies* 32 (6): 603–619.

Hong, Won-Pyo. 2010. "Multicultural Education in Korea: Its Development, Remaining Issues, and Global Implications." *Asia Pacific Education Review* 11: 387–395.

Hundt, David, Jessica Walton, and Elishia Lee. 2019. "The Politics of Conditional Citizenship in South Korea: An Analysis of the Print Media." *Journal of Contemporary Asia* 49 (3): 434–451.

Kang, Soon-won. 2010. "Multicultural Education and the Right to Education of Migrant Children in South Korea." *Educational Review* 62: 287–300.

Kim, Hyun Mee. 2007. "The State and Migrant Women: Diverging Hopes in the Making of 'Multicultural Families' in Contemporary Korea." *Korea Journal* 47 (4): 100–122.

Kim, Joon K. 2011. "The Politics of Culture in Multicultural Korea." *Journal of Ethnic and Migration Studies* 37: 1583–1604.

Kim, Hyun Mee. 2012. "The Emergence of the 'Multicultural Family' and Genderized Citizenship in South Korea." In *Contested Citizenship in East Asia: Developmental Politics, National Unity, and Globalization*, edited by Kyung-Sup Chang and Bryan S. Turner, 203–217. London: Routledge.

Kim, Stephanie K, and Lupita H. R. Kim. 2012. "The Need for Multicultural Education in South Korea." In *The Immigration and Education Nexus: A Focus on the Context and Consequences of Schooling*, edited by David A Urias, 243–253. Rotterdam: Sense Publishers.

Korean Educational Statistical Service (KESS). 2014. "Basic Statistics on Schools: Multicultural Students." Accessed September 10, 2015. http://kess.kedi.re.kr/eng/publ/publFile/pdfjs?survSeq=2014&menuSeq=3894&publSeq=2&menuCd=62384&itemCode=02&menuId=1_3_14&language=en.

Korean Statistical Information Service (KOSIS). 2015. "Current Status of Foreign Residents by the Local Government." Accessed January 15, 2018. http://kosis.kr/eng/statisticsList/statisticsList_01List.jsp#SubCont.

Lee, Hye-Kyung. 2008. "International Marriage and the State in South Korea: Focusing on Governmental Policy." *Citizenship Studies* 12 (1): 107–123.

Lee, Claire Seugeun. 2017. "Narratives of 'Mixed Race' Youth in South Korea: Racial Order and In-Betweenness." *Asian Ethnicity* 18 (4): 522–542.

Lentin, Alana. 2005. "Replacing 'Race': Historicising the 'Culture' in Multiculturalism." *Patterns of Prejudice* 39 (4): 379–396.

Lie, John, ed. 2015. *Multiethnic Korea? Multiculturalism, Migration, and Peoplehood Diversity in Contemporary South Korea*. Berkeley: Institute of East Asian Studies.

Lim, Timothy. 2010. "Rethinking Belongingness in Korea: Transnational Migration, 'Migrant Marriages' and the Politics of Multiculturalism." *Pacific Affairs* 83 (1): 51–71.

Ministry of Gender Equality and Family (MOGEF). 2008. *Damunhwakajokjiwonbeop* [Multicultural Families Support Act]. Accessed March 20, 2018. http://www.law.go.kr/engLsSc.do?tabMenuId=tab45&query=%EB%8B%A4%EB%AC%B8%ED%99%94%EA%B0%80%EC%A1%B1%EC%A7%80%EC%9B%90%EB%B2%95#.

Moon, Seungho. 2010. "Multicultural and Global Citizenship in the Transnational Age: The Case of South Korea." *International Journal of Multicultural Education* 12 (1): 1–15.

Noble, Greg. 2005. "The Discomfort of Strangers: Racism, Incivility and Ontological Security in a Relaxed and Comfortable Nation." *Journal of Intercultural Studies* 26 (1–2): 107–120.

Noble, Greg. 2011. "'Bumping Into Alterity': Transacting Cultural Complexities." *Continuum: Journal of Media & Cultural Studies* 25 (6): 827–840.

Paik, Young-Gyung. 2010. "'Not-Quite Korean' Children in 'Almost Korean' Families: The Fear of Decreasing Population and State Multiculturalism in South Korea." In *New Millenium South Korea: Neoliberal Capitalism and Transnational Movements*, edited by Jesook Song, 130–141. New York: Routledge.

Radford, David. 2016. "'Everyday Otherness': Intercultural Refugee Encounters and Everyday Multiculturalism in a South Australian Rural Town." *Journal of Ethnic and Migration Studies* 42 (13): 2128–2145.

Shin, Gi-Wook. 2006. *Ethnic Nationalism in Korea: Genealogy, Politics and Legacy*. Palo Alto: Stanford University Press.

Shin, Gi-Wook, James Freda, and Gihong Yi. 1999. "The Politics of Ethnic Nationalism in Divided Korea." *Nations and Nationalism* 5 (4): 465–484.

Smith, Greg. 2005. *Children's Perspectives on Believing and Belonging*. London: National Children's Bureau for Joseph Rowntree Foundation.

Walton, Jessica. 2018. "'I am Korean': Contested Belonging in a 'Multicultural' Korea." In *Interrogating Belonging for Young People in Schools*, edited by Chris Halse, 113–140. London: Palgrave Macmillan.

Walton, Jessica. Forthcoming. "Affective Citizenship and Peripheral Intimacies: Children's Inter-Ethnic Relations in South Korean Schools'." *Anthropology & Education Quarterly*.

Watkins, Megan. 2011. "Complexity Reduction, Regularities and Rules: Grappling with Cultural Diversity in Schooling." *Continuum: Journal of Media & Cultural Studies* 25: 841–856.

Watson, Iain. 2012. "Paradoxical Multiculturalism in South Korea." *Asian Politics and Policy* 4: 233–258.

Wise, Amanda, and Selvaraj Velayutham. 2009. "Introduction: Multiculturalism and Everyday Life." In *Everyday Multiculturalism*, edited by Amanda Wise, and Selvaraj Velayutham, 1–17. London: Palgrave Macmillan.

Everyday multiculturalism in union: power construction in migrant domestic workers' unionism

Raees Begum Baig ⓘ

ABSTRACT

Migrant domestic workers are often excluded from government policies due to their lack of citizenship. Such exclusion positions migrant domestic workers at the bottom of the social and political power structure. However, research has found that, with the establishment of unions, everyday interactions among local and migrant domestic workers have strengthened; which has not only enhanced understanding between locals and migrants, but also broken the ethnic and migration status power structures. The reconstruction of power coincides with the concepts of power in everyday multiculturalism. Through exploring the involvement of Nepalese migrant domestic workers in the union movement, this paper seeks to uncover how everyday multiculturalism reconstructs power structures for local and migrant domestic workers and builds a community of interdependence among domestic workers. This discovery gives insights into the role of union and labour activists in facilitating everyday multiculturalism, which has not been previously explored.

Introduction

Migrant domestic workers (MDWs) are believed to be the most vulnerable group of all migrant workers due to the working condition in a domestic setting (Mullally and Murphy 2014; ILO 2016). Domestic work settings involve MDWs performing domestic duties in the household of the employer. Limited mobility and confinement often cause MDWs to be socially excluded, marginalized and abused (Mullally and Murphy 2014; Islam and Cojocaru 2016). Female MDWs are subjected to physical and psychological abuse, sexual harassment and discrimination due to their vulnerable identities as female low-skilled labour (Islam and Cojocaru 2016). The limited protections and rights from both sending and receiving countries subject MDWs to institutional discrimination and exclusion (Dwyer and Papadimitriou 2006).

Hong Kong, as a predominately Chinese society, has a history of ethnic minority settlement since the early British colonial days. In Hong Kong, ethnic minorities are persons who report themselves as non-Chinese in the population census. Ethnic minorities and their families, mainly from India, Pakistan and Nepal, who worked for the British colonial government, were granted the right of abode in Hong Kong before the change of sovereignty from the United Kingdom to China in 1997. In the 1980s, MDWs from South and Southeast Asian countries, mainly the Philippines and Indonesia, started to work in Hong Kong. Intense discrimination and racism are experienced by minorities in everyday living in Hong Kong, including by Filipino and Indonesian MDWs (Research Office Legislative Council Secretariat 2017). However, unlike local ethnic minority residents, MWDs face double exclusion from both the ethnic minority and majority Chinese populations because they are not citizens. Such exclusion is constructed by the government under the visa policy for MDWs.

In order to empower MDWs in Hong Kong, local unionists have assisted in establishing the Hong Kong Federation of Asian Domestic Workers' Unions (FADWU). FADWU was established in 2010 with assistance from Hong Kong Confederation of Trade Unions (HKCTU) and other local labour rights organizations. The unionists hoped that through the establishment of FADWU, domestic workers would have a venue to understand each other and to advocate for their labour rights through collective action. Through interaction and communication between domestic workers from different ethnic backgrounds, these workers could have a better understanding of others' working conditions, which could enhance collectiveness and increase their political power in negotiating with the government, MDWs have limited political rights in Hong Kong because they are not citizens.

Everyday multiculturalism was initially developed to understand the group dynamics between host populations and newcomers in constructing multicultural interactions and relationship building (Wise 2010; Watson and Saha 2012; Shan and Walter 2015). Recognizing the construction of multiculturalism as a bottom-up process with attention to on-the-ground interactions, everyday multiculturalism challenges the state's top-down process in constructing multiculturalism which generates a power hierarchy.

Through exploring the involvement of Nepalese MDWs in the union movement, this paper examines how everyday multiculturalism in labour unions reveals the reconstruction of power structure among Nepalese MDWs and domestic workers of various ethnicities. It was found that Nepalese MDWs, the most powerless group due to their small population and lack of citizenship, were empowered through interactions with local workers in the labour movement and subsequently advocate for their rights. This research further found that the recognition of differences among MDWs of various ethnic backgrounds uncovered through everyday cross-cultural interactions helped to bind groups of domestic workers together and even strengthened their interdependence. Such informal connections and interdependence breaks the power hierarchy constructed by the government.

Transnational female labour movement in Hong Kong

The economic development in the late 1970s meant more middle-class families in Hong Kong were able to afford hiring MDWs. To respond to the large-scale influx of MDWs, immigration policy was made to allow MDWs to work in Hong Kong. Starting in the 1970s, MDWs mainly from Southeast Asian countries came to Hong Kong to work. In 2017, there were 359,651 MDWs in Hong Kong, 201,096 Filipinos and 159,613 Indonesians, accounting for more than 4 per cent of the whole population and more than half the ethnic minority population (HKSAR Census and Statistics Department 2017). Filipinos arrived in Hong Kong in the 1980s, followed by the Indonesians in the 1990s (Constable 2007). MDWs from other South and Southeast Asian countries, such as India and Nepal, have also been increasing in number for the past 10 years.

Social and political exclusion of MDWs

The rights and obligations of MDWs are established by the HKSAR government in the Standard Employment Contract (ID 407), the Employment Ordinance and the Immigration Ordinance. As the Standard Employment Contract is specifically applicable to MDWs, it is believed that the terms subject MDWs to higher vulnerability and social and political exclusion compared with the rights and obligations of other migrant workers (Mission for Migrant Workers 2013).

The compulsory "live-in policy" and the "2-week rule" are requirements applicable solely to MDWs. These conditions of stay have been controversial and have been criticized for subjecting MDWs to be highly vulnerable. Under Clause 3 of the Standard Employment Contract, MDWs are required to live with the employer (i.e. the "live-in policy"). Such a requirement causes MDWs to be highly regulated by the employer due to proximity, living space, and working hours and even subjected to various forms of abuse by the employer. A study conducted on 1,000 MDWs found that the average working hours for MDWs in Hong Kong is 11.9 per day, and two-thirds of the respondents reported that they have been working more than 12 h per day (Justice Centre Hong Kong 2016). Another study by the Equal Opportunities Commission found that at least 6.5 per cent of the interviewed MDWs have experienced sexual abuse by their employer in the premise (Equal Opportunities Commission 2014). Another study found that 58 per cent of MDWs have experienced verbal abuse and 18 per cent experienced physical abuse (Mission for Migrant Workers 2013).

Furthermore, according to the Section 2(4) of the Immigration Ordinance, MDWs are excluded from becoming permanent residents in Hong Kong. As implied in their visa condition, under the New Condition of Stay policy, a MDW is only allowed to stay in Hong Kong for at most 2 weeks after the contract completion or termination (the "2-week rule") (HKSAR Immigration Department 2015). This is to disrupt the continuity for MDWs, to prevent them from fulfilling the 7-years requirement to apply for permanent residency (Chen and Szeto 2015).

These conditions mean MDWs have the least social and political power in Hong Kong society and greatly restricts them from social and political participation. Article 26 of the Basic Law stipulates that "Permanent residents of the Hong Kong Special Administrative Region shall have the right to vote and the right to stand for election in accordance with law" (HKSAR Government 2019). Without the right to obtain permanent residency, formal political power granted by the government is severely limited.

The lack of permanent residency status differentiates MDWs from the local ethnic minority population. Although MDWs are categorized as part of the ethnic minority population under government data from the Census and Statistics Department, the policy directives of the Hong Kong Special Administrative Region (HKSAR) government towards ethnic minority permanent residents and MDWs are differentiated; policies regarding ethnic minority permanent residents focus on social integration, and policies are more on labour rights protection for MDWs (HKSAR Office of the Chief Executive 2018).

Exclusion from the policy formulation on multiculturalism

The race relations policy stipulates the HKSAR government's position on multiculturalism. Formulated alongside the consultation document on legislating against racial discrimination in 2004, the government's policy on race relations is: (a) to eliminate and combat all forms of racial discrimination; (b) to promote racial equality and communal harmony; and (c) to encourage ethnic minorities in Hong Kong to integrate into the wider society, while retaining their cultural identity (the integration policy). The integration policy comprises three elements: (a) to provide practical assistance to members of ethnic minorities to facilitate their settlement in Hong Kong and their integration into the wider community; (b) to address the problem of racial discrimination against ethnic minorities; and (c) to promote equal opportunities for all ethnic groups (HKSAR Home Affairs Bureau 2004).

Although MDWs are part of the ethnic minority population, they were excluded from the policy formulation process and their rights are not addressed in these policies (HKSAR Legislative Council 2006). These policies were formulated by the government with input from members of the Committee on the Promotion of Racial Harmony (CPRH) which consists of members from civil society and government officials. The committee was formed to advise the government on public education and publicity to promote racial harmony. The non-official civil society members were considered representatives from ethnic minority communities based on their experience in race-related work, and they were expected to act as a bridge between the government and ethnic minority communities (HKSAR Race Relations Unit 2017).

The top-down, policy-driven appointment of the advisory body retained an existing hierarchical power structure across ethnic groups. Non-official members are not elected by ethnic minority groups as representatives but are appointed by the government. Their representativeness is also questionable: many are from a prestigious social class with high education attainment and economic status. Additionally, because of the minimal participation of migrant women, concerns about gender equality and the rights of MDWs were not on the agenda of CPRH (HKSAR Race Relations Unit 2016). Specific conditions experienced by MDWs, including the "live-in policy" and the "2-week rule", were not covered by the anti-racial discrimination legislation; however, the United Nations Committee on the Elimination of Racial discrimination considers these conditions highly discriminatory, as they only apply to MDWs, and has repeatedly condemned the HKSAR government for not protecting MDWs from discrimination under these conditions (UNCERD 2009).

Multiple vulnerabilities of Nepalese MDWs

Nepalese MDWs are perceived to be the most invisible population. Unlike the Filipino and Indonesian MDWs, who constitute more than 90 per cent of the MDWs population, there were only around 1,000 Nepalese MDWs in Hong Kong in 2015, and visa applications for MDWs from Nepal have been suspended since 2015 for security reasons (HKSAR Census and Statistics Department 2015; HKSAR Labour and Welfare Bureau 2015).

Filipino and Indonesian domestic workers have formed strong unions and labour rights organizations in Hong Kong that have deep connections with local unions, religious groups and civil society (Constable 2007). These organizations strengthen Filipino and Indonesian MDWs' social and political power through collective action to advocate for MDWs' rights.

Nepalese MDWs are relatively new in Hong Kong. As a small population lacking familiarity in Hong Kong due to limited connection with local unions and other MDWs groups, Nepalese MDWs often have a lower level of awareness about their working conditions and rights. This means they face more serious exploitation and exclusion than other MDWs, including overwork, underpay, lack of job security and visa ban (Constable 2007; UNIFEM 2009). A survey conducted in 2016 found that almost half the Nepalese MDWs were underpaid and more than half did not receive the statutory rest hour (Catherine Lai 27 September 2016). Unionists attributed the reason for the serious exploitation experienced by Nepalese workers to the lack of public interest in the situation of these workers.

To protect the labour rights of Nepalese MDWs, the Union of Nepalese Domestic Workers in Hong Kong (UNDW) was established in 2005 by a few Nepalese MDWs and local unionists from the Hong Kong Confederation of Trade Unions (HKCTU) and the International Domestic Workers Federation (IDFW) (Union of Nepalese Domestic Workers 26 July 2005). Affiliated to FADWU, Nepalese MDWs gain more opportunity to interact with local domestic workers and workers of other ethnicities.

The concept of power in everyday multiculturalism

Power exists in all forms of social relationship. The socially constructed nature of power across individuals and groups leads to understanding how an individual's perceptions of reality can construct and reconstruct power structures. Although The Social Construction of Reality developed by Peter Berger and Thomas Luckmann (1989) does not explicitly state the concept of power, Dreher believes the concepts of the interconnectivity of objective reality and subjective reality in The Social Construction of Reality are highly relevant to the phenomenon of power (Dreher 2016).

According to the "dialectic relationship between objective and subjective reality" in The Social Construction of Reality, subjective meanings are given to objective facts that construct the subjective reality. Dreher relates this to the concept of power, as power structures and hierarchies are structural but under constant subjective interpretation (Dreher 2016). Institution, as a form of social control constructed through human action, generates power differences in order to exert the duty of social control on human conduct, and power structure and hierarchies are thus constructed by institutions as objective reality. However, although such institutionally constructed power structure and hierarchies are embedded in the process of socialization, people's understanding of these established power structures (subjective reality) depends on their knowledge of society and their social status, which helps them to interpret the institutionally constructed structure (Dreher 2016).

The state as a formal institution plays a dominant role in constructing racial power. The granting of citizenship by the state creates power differences, as it determines the social and political meaning of membership of the society. Non-citizens are regarded are excluded from such membership and rights attached to it. The formulation of the multiculturalism policy by the state which governs racial interaction also constructs the racial power structure. Multiculturalism has been criticized as premised on nation-based citizenship so that non-citizen migrants are often excluded from multicultural policy (Shan and Walter 2015). Furthermore, an uneven distribution of power exists between groups of the dominant culture and migrants, as well as within migrant groups. The formulation of a multicultural policy has been criticized as mainly dominated by middle-class politicians and elites (Hage 1998; O'Connor 2010; Meer 2015). The concept of multiculturalism in a society reflects the ideals of the politicians and elites in constructing the society. In a civil democratic political system, the ability of migrants and minorities to be included in the policymaking structure depends on their citizenship and political power and awareness. The granting of citizenship by the state reflects the selection of membership through controlling who should be admitted (Baig 2012). The lack of citizenship and the differences in migration status largely affect migrants' and minorities' political power so that they are often excluded from multicultural policymaking processes. Even if they have equal citizenship, barriers such as language, political awareness and interest and cultural values may hinder them from participating in policymaking (Baig 2012).

However, similar to Dreher's idea of power in The Social Construction of Reality, everyday multiculturalism does not see institutionally constructed objective power structure as uncontested; subjective interpretation and negotiation of power differences on the society level continuously construct and reconstruct the power structure. One key aspect of the development of an everyday multiculturalism concept is to challenge this unequal power structure through acknowledging the fact that contemporary multicultural society is not a collective of "equal diversities" but groups constituted through power relations (Colombo 2015). Interactions and negotiations of groups and individuals are made in a space of power and social inequalities. Rather than seeing multiculturalism from a top-down perspective, everyday multiculturalism addresses the disconnection between political ideal and day-to-day reality by focusing on the everyday interactions of people. By focusing on grounded everyday interactions, citizenship can be understood from the bottom-up as people express their citizenship through claiming their rights and fighting for recognition (Watson 2009; Colombo 2015).

Framework for this study

As an analytical framework, everyday multiculturalism stresses the interplay between the micro and macro conditions to uncover the ways that construct and reconstruct racial power differences to demand inclusion and contest the state's formulated power dynamic which generates segregation (Butcher and Harris 2010; Colombo 2010). In order to contest the state-constructed power structure and negotiate differences among racial groups, everyday practices of intercultural encounters and exchange are needed (Butcher and Harris 2010).

In addition to the power difference between the state and the society levels, it is important to recognize the power relationships between the dominant cultural group and migrant groups, and among individuals within the same migrant group. Power differences are situated differently in every space, each space shapes cultural difference in particular ways (Amin 2002). Every society or space has a normative moral power that leads to both inclusion and exclusion such as discrimination. Levels of acceptance and tolerance within cross-cultural spaces are unevenly distributed (Wise 2007). This could be due to racism and other forms of discrimination but also to a lack of understanding. Drawing on Wise's concept (Wise 2007), the role of "transversal enablers" becomes crucial in bringing together different groups to educate each other about the differences in cultural norms and practices. Transversal enablers not only bridge the dominant and migrant groups but should be aware of the power differences between both sides and break the power structure.

This study applied the analytical framework of everyday multiculturalism to power to examine the reconstruction of power through intercultural interaction between Nepalese MDWs and local domestic workers in the union. The framework of this study focuses on the interplay between the micro and macro conditions in reconstructing power dynamics. The micro condition is the everyday interaction practice between Nepalese MDWs and local domestic workers in the union that allows negotiation on differences to take place; the macro condition is the state construction of racial power hierarchies including citizenship and social and political inclusion. Looking at the interconnectivity of the top-down and bottom-up approaches in power construction, the framework uncovered the ways and factors that facilitate the intercultural interaction and negotiation of differences between Nepalese MDWs and local domestic workers, to reconstruct the power structure.

Research methodology

This article draws on a larger research project that examined the capacity and agency of migrant workers' activism in Hong Kong and South Korea between February and June 2016. The study aimed to explore the capacity of migrant workers and their unions to advocate for migrant workers' rights and protection through collective actions. In this article, I focus on the experiences of Nepalese MDWs in Hong Kong. Drawing on their experiences in Hong Kong and interactions with local domestic workers, this article analyses how ethnicity and migration status of Nepalese MDWs influence their day-to-day cross-cultural interactions with local workers and their participation in labour movements.

Six semi-structured interviews were conducted with stakeholders from Nepalese MDWs, local Chinese domestic workers, local unionists and local

Table 1. Overview of individual interview participants.

Name	Age range	Ethnicity	Position
Chunni	40s	Nepalese	Migrant domestic worker, Chairperson of UNDW
Bindu	30s	Nepalese	Migrant domestic worker, Executive committee member of UNDW
Bobo	50s	Hong Kong Chinese	Local domestic worker, Former chairperson of HKDWGU
Fly	40s	Hong Kong Chinese	Labour unionist of HKCTU
Leo	20s	Hong Kong Chinese	Labour unionist of HKCTU
Fish	30s	Hong Kong Chinese	Labour unionist of IDWF

Nepalese; including two Nepalese MDWs who were also the chairperson and vice chairperson of the UNDW, a local Chinese domestic worker who was the ex-chairperson of the Hong Kong Domestic Workers General Union (HKDWGU), and three local Chinese labour activists working in the HKCTU and the International Domestic Workers Federation (IDWF). A focus group was also conducted with eight female Nepalese MDWs. Table 1 gives a basic overview of the individual interview participants.

Ethical approval was applied and granted by the Survey and Behavioural Research Ethics Faculty Sub-committee of the Faculty of Social Sciences, the Chinese University of Hong Kong. Each interviewee in both individual and focus group interviews was given a consent form to sign. The consent form included a detailed description of the research background and the ways to make enquiry and complaint regarding any possible maltreatment during the course of interview. Interviewees needed to indicate their willingness to use their provided names in any documentation of the research and to audio record the interview for internal usage of the research team. Upon their consent, interviews with the Nepalese MDWs were conducted in English and in Chinese with the local Chinese interviewees, all interviews took place in the offices of their corresponding unions. Each interview lasted for 1.5 to 2 hours and was audio recorded. Data were transcribed after the interviews for further analysis.

Guiding questions were formulated according to the framework for individual and focus group interviews. The questions were used to explore the space and capacity for interethnic interactions within union setting, the perceived power structures and hierarchies among union members of different ethnic backgrounds, the role of the local unionists in facilitating the interethnic interactions, collaborative actions and solidarity building among unions on labour rights advocacy, and the institutional and public influences shaping interethnic interactions.

Participant observations were also carried out through attending major events organized by UNDW, including the annual general meeting and the weekly gatherings. These were conducted in order to uncover the patterns of interactions among different stakeholders through observing of their activities and the use of speech in their conversations.

Thematic analysis was used to analyse the data collected from individual and focus group interviews. Themes were set according to the framework and the guiding questions. Electronic coding was proceeded after the transcriptions were ready by Nvivo. The nodes generated were then gone through manually to countercheck and validate the matching of the themes and transcripts.

Union as a space for cross-ethnic interaction

Interactions across social and ethnic classes have never been easy. Amin (2002) attributed ethnic and class tensions to the dominant ethnic group's threat to migrant workers. The succession of migrant settlement or the influx of migrant workers, especially migrants are of different cultural backgrounds and economically deprived, challenges the working class of the dominant ethnicity for their job security and cultural unity. The dominant group feels a loss of ethnic supremacy and opportunities compared to before increased migration. When migrant workers start to claim rights, such tensions between local and migrant working classes became even more serious (Gonzalez-Sobrino 2016).

In order for migrants to build momentum to make claims of their rights as domestic workers, a space for social interactions between ethnic groups is crucial. Although street-level interaction among the working class of the dominant ethnic group and migrants is minimal, my research found that unions, as a kind of micropublic, helped to facilitate inter-ethnic interactions. A micropublic is a space where engagement across cultures could be found (Amin 2002; Ho 2011). Such common space allows social contacts that are important for reconciling and overcoming cultural differences (Amin 2002).

Labour movements organized by MDWs in Hong Kong started in the 1980s. Early movements were characterized by unions, formed according to ethnicity with strong transnational connections to unions in their home countries. However, as these MDW union memberships are based on ethnicity, they have weak connections with the local labour movement, which makes them unable to gain local support to advocate for their rights and lobby the government. Seeing the government cares little about the abuses experienced by MDWs, including overwork and underpay, the HKCTU proposed to set up an official federation of all domestic workers' unions in Hong Kong in order to foster collective bargaining for MDWs, and FADWU was established in 2010 (ILO 2012). With the local domestic workers' union, HKDWGU, being a founding member of FADWU, and affiliated to HKCTU, MDWs started to have more spaces to interact with local workers and migrant workers from other ethnic backgrounds. The inclusion of different ethnic-based unions in HKCTU opened up a space to not only facilitate ethnic interactions, but also successfully breakdown the ethnic and gender power structures.

Reconstructing power through negotiating everyday otherness

With the help of HKCTU, local and MDWs jointly formed FADWU based on their shared identity as domestic workers. Because of this shared identity and joint affiliation, migrant and local domestic workers felt obliged to show solidarity with each other. However, the physical setting of the space did not necessarily generate communication; instead, specific barriers hindered cross-ethnic interaction including ethnic differences and inability to communicate well with each other due to language barriers. The perception held by local domestic workers towards MDWs that MDWs were coming to Hong Kong to steal their jobs further hindered social interaction. Bobo, the former chairperson of HKDWGU, claimed that with "solidarity" as the core value of the labour movement, local domestic workers tried to support MDWs; yet true solidarity was hard to build. During the early days, after FADWU was formed, local domestic workers were very sceptical towards MDWs. As Bobo said:

> Actually, if I say our members supported MDWs, then I must be lying. Many of our sisters think that they come to steal our jobs. Previously we have lots of domestic work we can do, child care, cleaning.

The sense of uncertainty was also found in the MDWs in FADWU. Chunni, from UNDW, felt uncertain towards working with local domestic workers in the early days due to language barriers:

> Our Chinese and English [is] not good. Others have better language. We don't know how to communicate with them and make them understand us. And we as a very small union, we don't know what we can do to take part in the movement.

However, such scepticism lessened as the local domestic workers began to understand the different situation MDWs were facing. As the chairperson of HKDWGU, Bobo needed to attend regular FADWU executive committee meetings together with the representatives from other MDW unions. Because of these meetings, Bobo gained better understanding of the situation of MDWs and recognized the "Otherness" between local and MDWs. She found that local workers and MDWs engaged in different employment markets, those employers preferring live-in helpers hire MDWs, and local workers mainly working for families that do not want someone to live with them and work on a part-time basis. Her increased understanding helped her to talk with the other members of HKDWGU and persuade them to support and build solidarity with the MDWs.

> Bobo: When you think more about it, then you will discover MDWs are actually different from us. Just like if a family needs us to be 24 hours standby, we cannot do that, that's why we need them to do this job. And some families do not prefer someone staying at their home, and that will be our job. So we are serving two

different markets ... when I started to explain to the sisters, then they will understand and slowly accept foreign domestic workers.

The acknowledgement of the condition of stay for MDWs further motivated the local workers to help MDWs. After gaining more understanding of the condition of Nepalese MDWs, local domestic workers were more aware of the differences in job nature and that the abuses experienced by Nepalese MDWs were severe. The local workers tried to associate the experience with their own gendered and cultural identities. Developing an understanding of sameness from otherness helped the local domestic workers to strongly identify with MDWs.

> Bobo: Our sisters started to sympathize them. You know, we are all women; we all work for this invaluable job. We know how it feels for not being able to be with your family and have to stay with some strangers. Actually they are so poor, leaving their family and come to so far alone. They are just like Chinese women when we were young. At that time Chinese women could not choose their husband. After you get marry then you need to stay with a family you have not met before. If that family does not treat you well, you will have no way to seek help.

Such perceived differences between the local and MDWs and the openness of local workers to interact with Nepalese MDWs also empowered Nepalese MDWs to be more engaging. Among all the MDW unions, Nepalese domestic workers are perceived to be the least vocal ones. Nepalese workers were afraid to speak up during the meetings due to their language proficiency, they also have relatively less understanding about Hong Kong's social and political situations compared with other MDWs. However, because of their weaker position, the local domestic workers did not see them as much as a "threat" to their employment when compared to MDWs from other ethnic groups with greater numbers, such as Indonesian and Filipino MDWs. Furthermore, because of a paternalistic view of the Nepalese MDWs as people with worse living conditions, the local workers were more enthusiastic about helping them. Because of this support and solidarity, Nepalese workers felt empowered and gradually became more vocal in advocating for their rights. Chunni and Bindu recognized the importance of having other unions' support which helped them to feel more confident talking about Nepalese workers' situation and needs.

> Chunni: Nepalese domestic workers have a lot of problems, like agency fee and being underpaid. But people in Hong Kong do not care as we are much weaker than the Filipinos and the Indonesians; they are more vocal in the media. We do not know how to speak in front of the media. So the locals know very well, they teach us how to use media, do survey, and make us visible in front of the media. That is very helpful.
> Bindu: Yes, they support us, they understand us and support us, for their best. Before I very afraid of speaking to people, now OK.

Equalling power through labour solidarity

"Everyday otherness" in recent everyday multiculturalism literature has a negative connotation. As suggested by Radford (2016, 2130), "everyday otherness" is "reflective of the way people come to terms with and negotiate the conscious and unconscious differences that members of different communities feel, see, experience, understand and interpret when interacting with one another, or when one is aware of the 'others' presence in the community". The perception of difference is indeed due to a lack of understanding and a lack of engagement with each other. Such differences very often are not neutral but carry a strong sense of devaluation and discrimination towards the other group. However, in my research, the recognition of differences actually helped to bind the two groups of domestic workers together and even strengthened their interdependence.

According to the Labour Ordinance, local and MDWs have different of minimum wages. Local workers are protected by the Statutory Minimum Wage of HK$34.5 per hour, working the same hours as MDWs, local workers could receive HK$10,350, whereas the MDWs' minimum allowable wage is HK$4,520 per month (HKSAR Labour and Welfare Bureau 2019). Due to the distinct difference of minimum wage, labour actions advocating for a minimum wage increment for these two groups of domestic workers used to be separated. However, through a recognition of "everyday otherness", they became supportive to each other as local workers did not feel threatened by Nepalese migrant workers, while still maintaining a similar gendered and classed domestic worker identity. For example, Bobo and Chunni explained:

> Bobo: We will join their actions. We try to put ourselves into their role and think about what would they face, and try to discuss with them by using their perspectives. You know about the government … they never give you what you want. If you ask for pay rise, they will never give you the amount you request for. So we will teach them these strategies. And like advocating for agency fee and live-out options, we are also advocating for similar issues, we also face high agency fee and low salary. We can draw similarities from these different actions. And we are all women, of course we need to help each other … Of course we will help them [Nepalese MDWs], you know this government won't talk to migrant workers, if we go to meet the government with them, the government will listen. HK$4000 salary for MDWs is so low, how to afford a living? Of course need to ask for salary increment for them [Nepalese MDWs].
>
> Chunni: Yes, we will join Labour Day protest, support local workers, because they support us also. The Labour Department always only offer to meet us on weekdays. We cannot go as we need to work and take care of children. The local workers would help us attend those meetings and help us express our problems to the government.

With the assistance from the local unionists on interpretation and simple body language, local and MDWs were able to communicate with each other. The recognition of otherness through communication in the micropublic of the union labour movement constructed a "community of conviviality" (Shan and Walter 2015). Conviviality denotes the "capacity to live together" (Wise and Noble 2016). As a key concept in understanding community formation and in explaining how and why people come together, the concept of conviviality is exceptionally important in explaining labour behaviour and solidarity. Under Durkheim's (1964) concept of division of labour, solidarity is the product of a division of labour in a differentiated society. It is a state of collective conscience, which is when people as individuals recognize the importance of connectivity and cooperation to make society function. Solidarity can be developed across individual differences in social coexistence. Understanding conviviality in the context of everyday multiculturalism denotes a state of interdependence and a mode of living together (Shan and Walter 2015). Shan and Walter (2015) further define "community of conviviality" as different from vivid everyday interaction, the construction of a community of conviviality is based on human needs, which could be specific to different places where people live together. In the case of my study, the community of conviviality formed by the local workers and MDWs was based on a strong need for labour rights advocacy for both local and migrant workers, rather than the result of only day-to-day coexistence in Hong Kong society. The presence of domestic workers in the micropublic is based on the recognition of labour identity and interdependency for strengthening their labour advocacy. However, instead of constantly drawing similarities with each other, they developed a strong recognition of the differences between local and MDWs. This recognition of otherness helped to build up cohesion among the two groups of domestic workers so that they moved from initially feeling skeptical and threatened (from the local workers' perspectives) or scared to interact (from the Nepalese migrant workers' perspectives) to developing a "community of conviviality" through shared need on labour rights advocacy.

Bridging the communities for empowerment

Key stakeholders helped to facilitate this community of conviviality. People of different cultures do not necessarily or naturally come together; rather there are some individuals that foster these interactions through social networks. Wise (2009) calls these special individuals "transversal enablers". Transversal enablers have an important role in establishing connections and building cross-cultural community by helping to bring people with diverse backgrounds together. To assist in the creation of connections across cultural differences, transversal enablers engage and facilitate in transversal practices, such as "gift exchange, intercultural knowledge exchange, creating opportunities for the production of cross-cultural embodied commensality, and the production of spaces of intercultural care and trust" (Wise 2007, 4).

Transversal enablers are usually members who belong to a community of conviviality and have previously benefited from intercultural social networking. However, in this study, I found that the local labour activists from HKCTU, who do not belong to ethnic minority communities, played the role of transversal enablers. Local labour activists not only initiated the formation of FADWU, which brought local and MDWs onto the same platform, they further built up spaces for intercultural exchange to enhance understanding among domestic workers through hosting different cross-cultural activities, such as day camps and cooking classes. These activities not only aimed at enhancing intercultural understanding but served as important venues for identity building and forming a sense of commonality among domestic workers. An interviewee from HKCTU, Fly, mentioned:

> At the beginning, it was very difficult for local and MDWs to echo with each other, they do not identify with each other, and even they see each other as rivals. But we believed that it is due to the lack of understanding. Actually they are advocating for issues which can draw similarities, such as minimum wage and agency fee. So we try to break down the misunderstanding on "stealing my rice bowl" by bringing them together and understand each other's situation. We organise day camps, overnight camps and other classes. So using the name of cultural exchange, we aim at building cohesion among the two groups.

Another interviewee from HKCTU, Leo, echoed the difficulties faced by local labour activists in organizing intercultural activities, but felt that building a common ground with equal participation among members was important because it could strengthen the advocacy power or both sides.

> Leo: It was not easy at all because of language differences. Nepalese community has a long history in Hong Kong, but our local workers have no chance to meet a Nepalese in their lives. There is absolutely lack of understanding. We serve as interpreters to facilitate their communication, and encourage them to use their simple language and even body language to communicate with each other … We have to ensure the weaker unions, such as UNDW, to be able to speak up in the meetings. It is very natural that the strong unions and the locals would dominate the discussions during meetings. But we need to build a more balanced platform, so we will set some rules and also we, as facilitators, would encourage the Nepalese to speak more.

As this shows, HKCTU recognized equal participation is crucial to break the power structures between stronger and weaker unions and to empower the weaker unions to stay in the community of conviviality.

Local labour activists taking up the role of transversal enabler challenges the fundamental idea of everyday multiculturalism that the beneficiaries of multicultural interaction are solely the members of specific ethnic minority communities. Although local labour activists do not necessarily belong to any ethnic communities, they are not completely detached from these communities as they are part of the collective labour movement. Local labour activists saw

FADWU as an important platform for MDWs in order to advocate for their rights. Since not all MDW unions are strong enough to work on their own, the local labour activists and the MDW unionists recognized the need for a mutually supportive platform that could help to strengthen those weaker unions. The UNDW has a weaker structure compared to other unions, thus other unions could serve as role models and assist UNDW's development; on the other hand, local unions could also benefit from intercultural interactions. Such cohesion building stems from a shared value of labour solidarity. The role played by local labour activists also expanded the idea of the intercultural beneficiary under everyday multiculturalism to include those who do not necessarily belong to particular organized ethnic communities but to a collective movement that crosses ethnic lines.

Conclusion

Because of their ethnicity and lack of citizenship, MDWs are in a position of double disadvantage in Hong Kong society. State-constructed race relations policy not only excludes MDWs, but further reinforces their disadvantaged position by denying them citizenship rights, which puts them in a powerless social position among all minority ethnic groups.

Without a strong commitment from the state to support ethnic integration, everyday inter-ethnic interactions become more significant when examining the patterns of interaction and relationships across ethnic groups. By focusing on power structures in everyday multiculturalism contexts such as unions, my study found that the power structure among ethnic groups could be reshaped and, through this, the Nepalese MDWs who were interviewed began to feel empowered because of these everyday interactions and negotiations with local domestic workers.

Everyday cross-cultural interactions not only enhance understanding among migrant groups, but also breakdown the ethnic and migration status power structures between locals and migrant workers. Such reconstruction of power coincides with concepts of power in everyday multiculturalism. Examining the interactions between local and Nepalese MDWs in a union setting reaffirms the ability of everyday multiculturalism to break down hierarchical power structures among ethnic groups. Intensified ethnic interactions with local domestic workers union and other MDWs unions empowered the Nepalese MDWs to advocate for their rights in solidarity with local workers. HKCTU and FADWU, as micropublic, were able to bond local and MDWs through placing the two groups in the same space where they could engage in intercultural exchange and gradually learn about each other's working situation. With mutual understanding and communication facilitated in the union setting, and through gaining knowledge and support from local domestic workers, Nepalese MDWs became more capable of participating in ethnically diverse union environments and began to advocate for their rights.

This article also offers new insight into the role of transversal enablers and the conditions for conviviality in the setting of an ethnically diverse union environment. Instead of two groups of migrant and local domestic workers initiating inter-ethnic interaction, the local Chinese labour activists took up the role of transversal enablers. Additionally, this article provides a refinement on the concept of conviviality. In relation to the concept of everyday multiculturalism, conviviality is based on the ability to establish interdependence through negotiating similarities among ethnic groups. However, the experience of local and MDWs showed that conviviality could be built upon the concept of everyday "otherness" rather than "sameness". It was because of the ability to identify differences between the two groups of domestic workers that bonding was eventually established.

Overall, these insights explain that there is no defined pattern of everyday multiculturalism. The examination of everyday multiculturalism should be contextualized and shaped according to the setting of different culturally constituted micropublics. Such flexibility expands the scope of the debate of everyday multiculturalism.

Disclosure statement

No potential conflict of interest was reported by the author.

ORCID

Raees Begum Baig ⓘ http://orcid.org/0000-0003-4008-7764

References

Amin, Ash. 2002. "Ethnicity and the Multicultural City: Living with Diversity." *Environment and Planning A* 34: 959–980.

Baig, Raees. 2012. "From Colony to Special Administrative Region: Ethnic Minorities' Participation in the Making of Legislation Against Racial Discrimination in Hong Kong." *Social Transformations in Chinese Societies* 8 (2): 173–200.

Berger, Peter L., and Thomas Luckmann. 1989. *The Social Construction of Reality: A Treatise in the Sociology of Knowledge.* New York: Anchor Books.

Butcher, Melissa, and Anita Harris. 2010. "Pedestrian Crossings: Young People and Everyday Multiculturalism." *Journal of Intercultural Studies* 31 (5): 449–453.

Chen, Yun-Chung, and Mirana M Szeto. 2015. "In-your-face Multiculturalism: Reclaiming Public Space and Citizenship by Filipina Immigrant Workers in Hong Kong." In *Worlding Multiculturalisms: The Politics of Inter-Asian Dwelling*, edited by Daniel P. S. Goh, 55–74. New York: Routledge.

Colombo, Enzo. 2010. "Crossing Differences: How Young Children of Immigrants Keep Everyday Multiculturalism Alive." *Journal of Intercultural Studies* 31 (5): 455–470.

Colombo, Enzo. 2015. "Multiculturalisms: An Overview of Multicultural Debates in Western Societies." *Current Sociology Review* 63 (6): 800–824.

Constable, Nicole. 2007. *Maid to Order in Hong Kong: Stories of Filipina Workers*. New York: Cornell University.

Dreher, Jochen. 2016. "The Social Construction of Power: Reflections Beyond Berger/ Luckmann and Bourdieu." *Cultural Sociology* 10 (1): 53–68.

Durkheim, Emile. 1964. *The Division of Labour in Society*. New York: The Free Press.

Dwyer, Peter, and Dimitris Papadimitriou. 2006. "The Social Security Rights of Older International Migrants in European Union." *Journal of Ethnic and Migration Studies* 32 (8): 1301–1319.

Equal Opportunities Commission. 2014. *Sexual Harassment and Discrimination in Employment – Questionnaire Survey for Foreign Domestic Workers*. Hong Kong: Equal Opportunities Commission.

Gonzalez-Sobrino, B. 2016. "The Threat of the "Other": Ethnic Competition and Racial Interest." *Sociology Compass* 10 (7): 592–602.

Hage, Ghassan. 1998. *White Nation*. Sydney: Pluto Press.

HKSAR Census and Statistics Department. 2015. *Labour Force Characteristic*. Accessed October 20, 2016. http://www.censtatd.gov.hk/hkstat/sub/gender/labour_force/.

HKSAR Census and Statistics Department. 2017. *Hong Kong 2016 Population By-Census Thematic Report: Ethnic Minorities*. Hong Kong: HKSAR Government.

HKSAR Government. 2019. *The Basic Law*. Hong Kong: HKSAR government.

HKSAR Home Affairs Bureau. 2004. *Legislating Against Racial Discrimination: A Consultation Paper*. Hong Kong: HKSAR Government.

HKSAR Immigration Department. 2015. *Employment as Foreign Domestic Helpers*. Accessed October 20, 2016. http://www.immd.gov.hk/eng/services/visas/immigration-entry-guideline.html.

HKSAR Labour and Welfare Bureau. 2015. *LCQ15: Foreign domestic helpers*. Accessed January 30, 2019. https://www.lwb.gov.hk/eng/legco/15042015_2.htm.

HKSAR Labour and Welfare Bureau. 2019. *Foreign Domestic Helpers (FDHs)*. Accessed January 30, 2019. http://www.labour.gov.hk/eng/plan/iwFDH.htm.

HKSAR Legislative Council. 2006. *Panel on Education: Education for Children of Ethnic Minorities*. LC Paper No. CB(2)2642/05-06(4).

HKSAR Office of the Chief Executive. 2018. *The Chief Executive's 2018 Policy Address*. Hong Kong: HKSAR Government.

HKSAR Race Relations Unit. 2016. *Meetings of the Committee on the Promotion of Racial Harmony*. Hong Kong: HKSAR Government. Accessed October 20, 2016. http://www.had.gov.hk/rru/english/aboutus/aboutus_cprh.html.

HKSAR Race Relations Unit. 2017. *About Us*. Accessed December 20, 2017. http://www.had.gov.hk/rru/english/aboutus/aboutus_cprh.html.

Ho, Christina. 2011. "Respecting the Presence of Others: School Micropublics and Everyday Multiculturalism." *Journal of Intercultural Studies* 32 (6): 603–619.

ILO. 2012. *The Hong Kong Federation of Asia Domestic Workers Unions – FADWU: A Case Study*.

ILO. 2016. *Expanding Social Security Coverage to Migrant Domestic Workers*. Geneva: ILO.

Islam, Rezaul M., and Stefan Cojocaru. 2016. "Migrant Domestic Workers in Asia: Transnational Variations and Policy Concerns." *International Migration* 54 (1): 48–53.

Justice Centre Hong Kong. 2016. *Coming Clean: The Prevalence of Forced Labour and Human Trafficking for the Purpose of Forced Labour Amongst Migrant Domestic Workers in Hong Kong*. Hong Kong: Justice Centre Hong Kong.

Lai, Catherine. 2016. "Almost Half of Nepalese Domestic Workers are Underpaid and Do Not Receive Holidays – Survey." *Hong Kong Free Press*, September 27.

Meer, Nasar. 2015. "Looking up in Scotland? Multinationalism, Multiculturalism and Political Elites." *Ethnic and Racial Studies* 38 (9): 1477–1496.

Mission for Migrant Workers. 2013. *Live-in Policy Increases Female MDW's Vulnerability to Various Types of Abuse.* Accessed March 3, 2017. http://issuu.com/mfmw/docs/primer_live-in_english.

Mullally, Siobhan, and Cliodhna Murphy. 2014. "Migrant Domestic Workers in the UK: Enacting Exclusion, Exemptions, and Rights." *Human Rights Quarterly* 36 (2): 397–427.

O'Connor, Paul. 2010. "Accepting Prejudice and Valuing Freedom: Young Muslims and Everyday Multiculturalism in Hong Kong." *Journal of Intercultural Studies* 31 (5): 525–539.

Radford, David. 2016. "'Everyday Otherness' – Intercultural Refugee Encounters and Everyday Multiculturalism in a South Australian Rural Town." *Journal of Ethnic and Migration Studies* 42 (13): 2128–2145.

Research Office Legislative Council Secretariat. 2017. *Poverty of Ethnic Minorities in Hong Kong.* HKSAR: Legislative Council.

Shan, Hongxia, and Pierre Walter. 2015. "Growing Everyday Multiculturalism: Practice-Based Learning of Chinese Immigrants Through Community Gardens in Canada." *Adult Education Quarterly* 65 (1): 19–34.

UNCERD. 2009. *Concluding Observations of the Committee on the Elimination of Racial Discrimination – People's Republic of China.* Geneva: United Nations.

UNIFEM. 2009. *An In-depth Study on the Realities and Concerns of Nepalese Domestic Workers in Hong Kong.*

Union of Nepalese Domestic Workers. 2005. *First General Meeting 26 July 2005.* Accessed October 20, 2016. http://ndwhk.blogspot.hk/.

Watson, Sophie. 2009. "Brief Encounters of Unpredictable Kind: Everyday Multiculturalism in Two London Street Markets." In *Everyday Multiculturalism*, edited by Amanda Wise and Selvaraj Velayutham, 125–139. Basingstoke: Palgrave Macmillan.

Watson, Sophie, and Anamik Saha. 2012. "Suburban Drifts: Mundane Multiculturalism in Outer London." *Ethnic and Racial Studies* 36: 2016–2034.

Wise, Amanda. 2007. *Multiculturalism From Below: Transversal Crossings and Working Class Cosmopolitans.* Sydney: Centre for Research on Social Inclusion, Macquarie University.

Wise, Amanda. 2009. "Everyday Multiculturalism: Transversal Crossings and Working Class Cosmopolitan." In *Everyday Multiculturalism*, edited by Amanda Wise, and Selvaraj Velayutham, 21–45. Basingstoke: Palgrave Macmillan.

Wise, Amanda. 2010. "Sensuous Multiculturalism: Emotional Landscapes of Inter-ethnic Living in Australian Suburbia." *Journal of Ethnic and Migration Studies* 36: 917–937.

Wise, Amanda, and Greg Noble. 2016. "Convivialities: An Orientation." *Journal of Intercultural Studies* 37 (5): 423–431.

Multicultural encounters in Singapore's nursing homes: a care ethics approach

Shirlena Huang ⓘ and Brenda S.A. Yeoh ⓘ

ABSTRACT
This paper adopts a care ethics lens to examine multicultural encounters in the institutional care space of nursing homes in Singapore. We focus on the interactions between foreign and local care workers of different nationalities and ethnicities in their interactions as they work alongside one another to take care of elderly residents, as well as in the time they spend together after working hours. Drawing upon qualitative data, we seek to understand the practices and processes of how different groups "do" care in negotiating the boundaries of diversity that characterize their everyday encounters. Providing a perspective from Singapore contributes to a more plural understanding of multicultural care ethics from a location outside the western world.

Introduction

In recent years, high levels of transnational migration have increased the heterogeneity of cultures in major cities to the extent that many have been described as spaces of "super-diversity", a term Vertovec (2007, 83) used "to capture a level and kind of complexity surpassing anything many migrant-receiving countries have previously experienced". Within this intense mix of ethnicities, languages, religions, regional and local identities, economic positions, social classes, legal statuses and so on, different groups of citizens and (im)migrants (learn to) live with one another. Scholars of migration and multiculturalism have argued that in "living with difference" (Valentine 2008), locals and migrants often end up "divided into two groups", wherein the latter group is "defined by its faults, devalued, susceptible to discrimination" vis-à-vis the locals who "embod[y] the norm and whose identity is valued" (Staszak 2008, cited in Radford 2016, 3). Exactly how various local and (im)migrant groups "negotiate the boundaries of diversity" in their everyday encounters with one another, however, remains unclear (Ye 2017, 1036).

Using the lens of care ethics, our paper aims to unpack the practices and processes of "boundary work" between these groups as they negotiate cultural diversity in their daily lives. Because care ethics pays attention to the relationality and dynamism in interactions, it allows for "a radical openness to the simultaneity of difference and similarity to deconstruct dominant discourses that essentialise minorities as only different" (Askins 2015, 473). It also focuses on the practice of care. As such, we apply care ethics to understand the everyday "doing of care" across ethnic and cultural boundaries in Singapore's nursing homes which, as we argue below, are everyday spaces of cultural diversity. We focus on the interactions and relationships between local and migrant care workers to first identify the work of boundary-making across culture, nationality and other dimensions in situations of conflict and cooperation; and second, to interrogate the possibilities of and limits to how reciprocity in care reshapes asymmetries of care relations and power across these boundaries.

The paper next considers the idea of encounters in the context of migration and multiculturalism, before discussing how a care ethics approach can enhance our understanding of the ways migrants and non-migrants negotiate intercultural encounters and interactions. We examine such interactions among foreign and local healthcare workers in the culturally-diverse environment of nursing homes in Singapore. In so doing, we highlight the usefulness of care ethics as a conceptual lens in studying everyday intercultural interactions given its emphasis on the dynamic and processual nature of subject positions, where individuals and groups are simultaneously negotiating the perceived boundaries that divide them, while also discovering dimensions of commonality that connect them.

Intercultural encounters in the global city

What does the diversity of the contemporary global city as "the very place of our meeting with the [cultural] other" (Jacobs 1996, 4) mean for life in cities today? While scholars agree that such encounters are profoundly about overcoming emotional struggles as people grapple with difference, there is less agreement regarding the outcome of these efforts. Baumann (2003, cited in Neal and Vincent 2013, 917) contends that perceptions of cultural differences in urban environments can result in either "mixophobia" (cultural withdrawal and avoidance) or "mixophilia" (where positive views of difference draw people to live in culturally diversified urban areas). But even mixophilia may remain at an abstract level and not necessarily translate into increased or meaningful social engagement between different groups.

Scholars have questioned the simplistic assumptions written into Allport's (1954) contact hypothesis that argues that the coming together of different cultures in the same space is expected to lessen prejudices and anxiety, resulting in the dissolution of cultural differences and allowing for intercultural dialogue as people engage in mundane acts of "doing togetherness" (Laurier and Philo 2002, cited in Valentine 2008) in public spaces. As Valentine (2008) counters, the assumption that engagement and contact between individuals of different ethnic and cultural groups will increase multicultural competencies and produce new convivialities is "potentially naïve" (p.325), as urban etiquette does not automatically "equate with an ethics of care and mutual respect for difference" (p.329). Multicultural living could, at best, simply represent co-existence, tolerance and civil inattention and, at the other extreme, (re)produce negative feelings, aggravate existing conflicts and (re)affirm prevailing prejudices (Clayton 2009; Radford 2016; Wilson 2011). Hence, scholars have increasingly emphasized the importance of finding common ground in everyday spaces to better understand the tenor of "living with difference".

Along this vein, some scholars have followed Amin (2002) and Wise (2014) in arguing that we need to move the focus away from theoretical debates about multiculturalism and discussions about national-level multiculturalist policies because these are often abstracted from real life experiences (Hardy 2014, 15). Instead, they encourage giving attention to "actually existing multiculturalism" (Uitermark, Rossi, and van Houtum 2005) by observing how ordinary people interpret group-based cultural difference and engage with diversity and asymmetries of power to make sense of each other and support the principles of fairness in the micro-spaces of everyday life (Frisina 2012, 840). This growing body of scholarship on "everyday multiculturalism" emphasizes the need to examine informal social interactions in the "doing" of multicultural encounters, where "differences are negotiated on the smallest of scales" (Wilson 2011, 635), "often in unpanicked and routine ways" across a range of urban localities and sites (Neal and Vincent 2013, 911). Such everyday interactions are thought to have meaning-making capacity and redemptive potential if people are able to move beyond difference to "recognize simultaneous similarity", leading to the development of "new relations that shift pre-existing stereotypes through some appreciation or experience of connection or commonality" (Askins 2015, 473; see also Wilson 2017). As such, this work focuses on the ways a diversity of people may find common ground to "discover each other as multifaceted, complex and interdependent" (Askins 2015, 476) in the process of "doing" everyday life grounded in the materiality and proximity of ordinary, human-scale spaces.

We argue that a care ethics approach can be applied productively to the study of interactions between diverse body-subjects. While multiculturalism recognizes and values cultural diversity and allows for the development of an inclusive civic identity, it continues to reify cultural categories, constructing groups as substantive entities; because of this, it leaves little room to accommodate shifting power relations, let alone challenge power asymmetries (Scuzzarello 2015). We next discuss the moral dimensions of a caring ethic before highlighting the value of applying care ethics to multiculturalism.

Care ethics and the "doing of care"

The earliest wave of care theorists such as Carol Gilligan and Nel Noddings writing in the 1980s saw moral frameworks as reflecting gendered differences, with men operating on an ethic of justice and rights in counter-position to women operating within an ethic of care and relationships (Featherstone and Morris 2012). Our take on care ethics aligns with the second wave of care theorists who "unpicked the necessary relationship between femininity and caring and refined notions of care" thereby demonstrating that care is not necessarily located in either the feminine or independent individual identities but is produced inter-subjectively in relation to others (Raghuram 2016, 515). As an ethic that posits a relational concept of persons, care ethics is well-positioned to understand how the complexities of interpersonal relations and the attendant moral dilemmas and emotions affect one's decisions and actions to care for others vis-à-vis oneself. We see a care ethics approach as sharpening our understanding of the transformative potential in negotiating difference in intercultural interactions through a focus on care *relations*. Because it is attentive to the dynamic openness of care interactions, it enables us to think about "the plurality of possibilities" (Bowden 1997, 12) of how "we learn from and listen to others, thus enabling us to better respond to their needs" (Ramdas 2016, 846).

In particular, we adopt Joan Tronto's understanding of care[1] as a practice grounded in the daily activities of life that "includes everything we do to maintain, continue and repair our 'world' so that we can live in it as well as possible" (Tronto 1993, 103). This emphasis on care as a practice resonates with the idea of everyday multiculturalism as a category of lived practices (as discussed earlier). For Tronto, care as a practice requires more than a disposition and/or intention to care; it is about following through on the thought to give and receive care. Neither is caring simple or banal as it requires knowhow and moral judgment. In an ideal situation, there are four overlapping phases of care, each characterized by a moral dimension of what constitutes good caring (Tronto 2001). First, "caring about" involves genuine *attentiveness*, or the ability to perceive articulated and unspoken needs in self and others; to do so "with as little distortion as possible … could be said to be a moral or ethical quality" (Tronto 2001, 62). Second, "caring for" involves the moral dimension of a willingness to take serious *responsibility* for identified needs by marshalling resources to meet them. Third, "caregiving" is the phase in which care tasks are successfully performed to meet the individualized physical, psychological, cultural and spiritual needs of the care recipient (and family). This phase requires knowledge and *competence* because "incompetent care is not only a technical problem, but a moral one". Fourth, "care receiving" considers the moral aspect of *responsiveness* of the care recipient to the care received. Responsiveness is complex because it shares the moral burden for care among care recipients, care-givers and those who are responsible for care. Responsiveness, or a lack of it, brings the caring process full circle because it demands more attentiveness.

By bringing to the forefront the moral dimensions – attentiveness, responsibility, competence and responsiveness – that are embedded in the practice of care, Tronto alerts us to the conscious decisions that are made around the everyday act of giving and receiving care. These moral dimensions become especially apparent when not all the needs of care recipients (differentiated by class, ethnicity and so on) can be simultaneously met, and decisions need to be made about which care needs are to be prioritized. There is also the question of how care-givers' need for self-care can be balanced against the needs of the care recipients (Tronto 2001). Significantly, in an institutional setting when care-givers may not always have the authority to control care schedules or activities (Bowden 1997), such friction and misalignments are often inevitable. Because care ethics understands care as a moral concept and takes the other's needs as the starting point for what must be done (Featherstone and Morris 2012), it recognizes that care interactions are not formulaic but are intentional and responsive to specific situations and moments, whether culturally-inflected or otherwise.

Care ethics can add to the scholarship on encounters and everyday multiculturalism through its focus on relationality and the interdependencies that exist at group *and* individual levels. Scuzzarello (2015) contends that in "advocating an attentive and responsive approach to the needs and claims of minority groups and of the individuals within them" (p.67), a care ethics approach to multiculturalism is able to challenge power asymmetries because it is sensitive to the context of the encounter; a caring multiculturalism allows for "transformative dialogue" that ideally enables the introduction of "new shared, narratives of belonging" (p.76) to replace antagonistic group constructions when both participants are willing to listen to the other person, and subsequently rethink and change their initial views.

We position the nursing home in Singapore as an institutional space of compelled intercultural encounters, in which an ethics approach may allow us to glean insights into the "doing of care" and the remaking of relationships across cultural boundaries. It is not only a multicultural space forged by neoliberal forces in an ageing society, but a space that will become increasingly common as societies across the world that are ageing rapidly turn to migrant labour to meet their eldercare needs.[2] As an institutional space where ethnicity and layered class hierarchies intersect with a segmented multinational labour force, the nursing home is also a site that presents an opportunity to observe how care relations develop despite conflicts and tensions among those who are culturally different and who start out as strangers. We seek to gain insights into the institutional arrangements (of nursing homes) that support relationships of power and inequality, along dimensions of gender as well as ethnicity, culture, class, and citizenship, and how a multicultural care ethics approach can provide a better understanding of the potential to dismantle power relations in intercultural interactions.

We agree with Green (2012, 3) that it is through their formal healthcare work that care workers develop caring relations through practising care; those open to growth learn to move from a distant relationship with their care recipients ("power-over-others") to one of mutual connection ("power-with-others"). Thus, although Tronto's ethic of care is usually applied to understanding care-givers and their relationship with those who receive their care, we focus on the relationships and reciprocities of care among care workers of different nationalities and ethnicities to understand the processes that enable them to move the care they provide beyond obligation-based ethics tied to their work duties, to responsibility-based ethics arising from an inter-subjective recognition of mutual care among colleagues. In other words, the transformative potential of a caring multiculturalism among those who formally practise care daily in the workplace may extend into other multicultural work and non-work settings. This recognizes that we are all care-givers and receivers in some way and that care is necessary for the conduct of daily life. Our analysis seeks to "render visible the care practices fundamental to human survival and flourishing" (Featherstone and Morris 2012, 14) in contexts of cultural diversity.

Theorisations of ethical care have been criticized as drawing on ideas of care from the Global North and western power structures (Hankivsky 2014; Raghuram 2016) although care and its practice are culturally and geographically variable. Parvati Raghuram has thus called for studies that challenge the existing conceptualisations of care as a universal practice by "recognizing multiplicity in care ethics or even multicultural care ethics" (Raghuram 2016, 513) and displacing it from "the unnamed white body" and its "implicit locatedness" in the Global North (Raghuram 2019, 7). Locating our study of Singapore is an attempt to engage with understandings of multicultural care ethics from a different place in the world.

Multicultural landscapes of eldercare in Singapore

To decrease the burden on state resources, Singapore has adopted a neoliberal approach to eldercare with a shift towards market regulation, greater dependence on community voluntarism and a transfer of care responsibilities to families. Like other countries experiencing rapid ageing, Singapore depends heavily on migrant care labour the city-state's growing care deficit. From the late 1960s, migration policy opened channels for recruiting foreign domestic workers to undertake gendered work such as childcare, eldercare and housework in the privatized sphere of the family. In the last three decades, mirroring the gendered substitution of care labour in the home, the state has also become increasingly dependent on the transnational care migration of mainly women from developing Asia to meet institutional needs for eldercare labour.

Up to 70 per cent of the 4,000 formal long-term care workers in Singapore are migrants from its less affluent Asian neighbours; approximately one-third of these foreign workers are registered nurses while the rest are healthcare attendants and nursing aides (Leung and Menon 2011). While the more skilled and qualified (registered/staff nurses) enter on an "S" work pass which enables them to bring in dependants, the majority (enrolled nurses, nursing aides and healthcare attendants) are recruited under a renewable work permit system which forbids accompanying dependants and ties them to particular employers. Most of the latter work in nursing homes where foreign workers comprise the bulk of the long-term care labour force because low-paying, labour-intensive care work attracts very few locals. Many experience downward occupational mobility (e.g. from staff nurses to enrolled nurses or nursing aides) because their credentials and qualifications are not recognized. They may also suffer from systematic patterns of discrimination by their employers (e.g. assigned less desirable work or enjoy only limited promotion prospects) because of their status as temporary migrant workers.

Foreign healthcare workers are part of the 1.4 million foreigners working in Singapore (Ministry of Manpower 2018) who in total constitute close to 30 per cent of Singapore's population (Department of Statistics 2017, 3). Despite their significant numbers, foreigners are officially excluded from the Singapore state's "Chinese-Malay-Indian-Other" (CMIO) model of multicultural policy that applies only to integrating its citizen population. On the one hand, CMIO-multiculturalism encourages the different local communities to interact in a common space while maintaining differences and boundaries between ethnic groups (Siddique 1989). On the other hand, while the CMIO policy is aimed at "pacifying the social anxieties of [resident] ethnic minorities" in the face of a Chinese majority citizenry (Ho 2019, 54), this is moot for the foreign workers who enter the nation-state as temporary, non-resident, contract workers with no or limited pathways to permanent residency. Although many of these healthcare workers share Singaporeans' ancestral ethnic roots (e.g. Chinese and Indian),[3] significant numbers do not (Filipino and Burmese). They are also differentiated from their Singapore colleagues along several dimensions. Beyond cultural customs, these vectors of difference include legal status (the workers are non-citizens with temporary work visas, in contrast to locals who enjoy citizenship rights), language (although English is the working language, not every is equally adept at it) as week as age and seniority (the workers are predominantly new graduates in their 20s, while their Singapore colleagues are often senior nurses in their 50s and 60s).

This mix of Singaporeans and foreigners characterizes many of Singapore's nursing homes.[4] We find the nursing home a particularly interesting site to study quotidian multicultural interactions because it is a space where almost all (80–90 per cent) the healthcare workers are foreigners, usually from the People's Republic of China (PRC), India, Myanmar, the Philippines, and Sri Lanka (Huang, Yeoh, and Toyota 2012). While a majority in numbers when homogenized as "foreign" (the proportions by specific nationalities vary with each nursing home), the top nursing positions in the nursing home are held by Singaporeans. The multiple hierarchies of difference which structure the workers' interactions among themselves create circumstances that are potentially ripe for misunderstandings, resentment and even discord across the local–foreign divide, as well as among the various migrant groups.

To understand how the healthcare workers negotiate these daily interactions in the nursing home in the course of carrying paid care work as well as after work hours, we employed a qualitative approach to "captur[e] the rich experiences and in-depth meanings of health and healthcare in everyday contexts" (Yantzi and Skinner 2009, 403). The research is based on site visits to nursing homes and semi-structured interviews (conducted in the language of the participants' choice, usually English for the Singaporeans, Filipinos and Indians, Mandarin for the Chinese and Burmese for those from Myanmar) with 35 foreign healthcare workers (13 from Myanmar; 11 from China, seven from the Philippines, and four from India) and seven Singaporeans working in a dozen nursing homes in Singapore.[5] Fieldwork was carried out by the authors and research assistants/translators in 2008–2010 and 2012–2013. Participants represented a variety of healthcare jobs (staff/registered nurses, enrolled nurses, nursing aides, healthcare attendants and physiotherapists) as well as the management of six nursing homes. The majority of the participants were women, with only five men (four foreigners and one local), consistent with the general profile of healthcare workers in Singapore. All workers are quoted using pseudonyms. In analyzing the transcripts, we paid attention to the actual conditions within which moral relations occur (Scuzzarello 2015, 75) and how "interconnectedness with others" (as indicated by utterances, feelings, activities) "influence ethical decision-making with regard to caring for others" (Green 2012, 1–2) and open up reflexive space among the workers. The qualitative approach enables us to "resist one-dimensional, passive objectifying constructions"

(Featherstone and Morris 2012, 10) of the participants while allowing us to understand them as individual knowable subjects, in keeping with a multicultural care ethics approach.

The possibilities and limits in learning to care across cultures

Examining care practice is an important part of understanding the ethical and moral dimensions of caring especially when such caring takes place in multicultural settings and situations that emphasize difference rather than acceptance. Cultural variations in training and understandings of care often result in workers geocoding and hierarchizing one another's competence along racial and national lines. Almost all the workers hold (at least initially) broad stereotypes, both positive and negative, of the other nationalities; for example, Filipino and PRC workers tend to initially regard those from Myanmar as extremely compassionate but lacking nursing skills, and Singaporean nurses generally regard those from the PRC as being technically skilled but less caring (Huang, Yeoh, and Toyota 2012). As observed by Raghuram (2019, 6), "the globalisation of the care industry brings together different groups of carers whose caring abilities are valued differently because of how their care is racialized". The foreign workers may also face prejudicial treatment from the nursing home residents and the latter's families; for example, some of the elderly are wary of being cared for by those who look different and speak in an unfamiliar language – what Black (2007, cited in Wilson 2011, 641–2) calls the effect of "visual play of skin" and "grammars of difference". Indeed, the large variety of accents (including Singlish[6]) add challenges to communication in English, especially of medical terminology, and institutional regulations prohibit them from falling back on their own languages. Further, unlike their Singapore colleagues who return home after work, foreign workers' off-work hours are often spent in close quarters with other colleagues, as many nursing homes require foreign staff to live on-site, usually housed four to a room with a deliberate mix of workers of different nationalities. This can also be the cause of problems because of cultural and personal differences (e.g. of how the space should be maintained).

Given the above, a sense of working harmoniously and happily together does not always happen naturally when healthcare workers, both foreign and local, first encounter one another in the space of the nursing home. This is not surprising because superficial interactions often reinforce, rather than counter, typecasting. However, those able to exercise a multicultural ethic of care, displaying the moral dimensions of attentiveness, responsibility, competence and responsiveness in their daily interactions, move towards dismantling power relations. Making an effort to see things from an inter-subjective position as well as seek out creative if often unremarkable ways to respond positively to one another's (perceived) differences, both in the course of their work and also beyond the contexts of work, generates opportunities for the development of meaningful relationships. As we go on to show, when parties are open to the possibility of and intentionally undertake multicultural learning even when success is not guaranteed, asymmetries of power and cultural differences can be overcome and care relations remade. When these possibilities are foreclosed, however, no transformative dialogue takes place and care relations are left unchanged.

Transformative possibilities

Even for those who choose to undertake paid care work, caring for one's colleagues does not necessarily come naturally, especially where markers of difference are highly visible and in action every day. Nonetheless, two important points are noteworthy about the workers' interactions. First, because care is processual and relational, it can be learnt through its practice. This was exemplified by Ling Ling (enrolled nurse, PRC, female) who had undertaken paid care work primarily as a means to earn a living. She said, "Having to do these things [manual tasks of physical care] made me learn more of the caring side. … I learnt how to care for the elderly patients. It's very hard to explain. … I also learnt patience". As Theresa, a Singaporean staff nurse with many years of nursing experience summarized, cultural differences – particularly with residents but also with colleagues – are not insurmountable "as long as they try to learn if they [already] don't know how to care". Second, as they carry out their daily care work among the residents, their interactions with one another foster care sensibilities among themselves. Even as she learnt to appreciate how to care for the residents, Ling Ling also learnt to appreciate her co-workers' ability to "do nursing care" well. She shared how she had observed her Burmese roommate regularly noticing residents who had "not been eating well" (in moral terms, this is showing attentiveness), worrying about them even after office hours and subsequently taking "her own initiative to call the family up and ask them why they haven't been visiting their elderly folk" (showing competence and taking responsibility). Not only did this admiration lead Ling Ling to praise her Burmese roommate and try to emulate her example (demonstrating responsiveness) of good care, she also became open to developing a cross-national friendship. Li Ying's case (nursing aide, PRC, female) also exemplifies the intersections between paid care work and collegial care. She described an incident in which a female Filipino nursing aide had a quick and skilful reaction to help a resident who was groaning in pain after falling from his wheelchair (attentiveness) while she (Li Ying) was too shocked to respond. This colleague not only checked the resident for vital signs and broken bones (competence) but also rallied the other nursing aides (including herself) into action, telling them to call the doctor-on-duty (responsibility). What her Filipino colleague had demonstrated has become for her the standard of nursing professionalism she now aspires towards (responsiveness).

Other workers were also able to develop new groupings of shared work identity that cut across ethnic and national boundaries, when they were open to new ideas and things. For example, Shao Lei (nursing aide, PRC, male) admitted that while he had not arrived easily at his current point of admiration for the Burmese, having a Burmese roommate who "always takes the initiative to ask me to teach him Mandarin" so they could communicate better, made him open to their intercultural friendship. It was because of this friendship that he now viewed "China healthcare workers [as] more like the Burmese – keen to learn and very serious in what we do". Personally feeling cared about, cared for, as well as being given and receiving care are also crucial to opening the door to positive intercultural experiences and reshaping social relations among the foreign workers. For example, Ji Wei (nursing aide, PRC, male) shared that two of his three best friends in Singapore are from Myanmar. Other than admiring their nursing care practice (particularly their "attention to the detail" and embodied intelligence such that even "for cases which other healthcare workers do not know what the dementia patients want … they can tell whether the patient is uncomfortable or needs the toilet"), Ji Wei shared how he personally benefitted when his Burmese roommate exercised these same dimensions of attentiveness, competence and responsibility with him. The latter had noticed how anxious and frightened Ji Wei was about working in "a completely new environment" when he first arrived (attentiveness). Ji Wei noted: "He not only helped me with work but also assured me that I would get used to things with time". His small group of best friends now regularly share meals as an intercultural experience: "Each of us will cook a dish from our hometown and we will eat together" (responsiveness). As Lachman (2012, 114) noted, "Caring weaves people into a network of relationships".

Thus, the rewards of successful intercultural interactions are more than just superficial exchanges. As Yi Fei (nursing aide, PRC, female) succinctly articulated: "I always tell my parents it's so unbelievable. All of us come from different countries, yet we are able to get along well and work together. We care for one another and I really feel like a community within this home". This demonstrates the workers' capacity to find dimensions of common ground over time through their everyday interactions. Ji Wei and Yi Fei are examples of the transformative potential of multicultural care ethics done right. Indeed, "it is through everyday spaces in which befriending occurs" (Askins 2015, 476) and those open to multicultural learning, create room for transformative dialogues that enable them to see past cultural differences, affirm one another's contributions and value, and even establish strong friendships across cultures and ranks.

Limited remaking

The more successful transformative remakings described above appear to characterize the interactions among the foreign workers rather than between the locals and foreigners. Perhaps their shared common identity as migrants unites them at some level; many of the foreigners – across job titles, nationality, gender and age – claimed that "nationality doesn't matter because we are all healthcare workers". In comparison, the most apparent differentials and asymmetrical power relations are between the locals and the foreign workers. Foreign healthcare workers are quick to realize early in their job appointments that not only do Singaporeans hold most of the senior nursing positions in a nursing home, but also that they are unwilling to do the dirty "hands on" aspects of eldercare and may sometimes be given a reduced share of such work. They also hear that locals are paid more for equivalent ranks. Such hierarchical positioning and what may be regarded as discriminatory practices can and do create barriers between the local and foreign workers. Dismantling these barriers – even in a limited way – requires persistence at practising ethical care.

Acknowledging that cultural gaps are expected "when you meet strangers", Singaporean Rosnah (Malay, nursing aide) emphasized that someone had to make the first move and how, as a local, it was her responsibility to do so "because if you don't approach them, they don't accept you". She shared how she goes about undoing the boundaries:

> You have to watch and see, watch and see. When it's safe, you must find time to be close with them, talk to them and make them understand [that] maybe they can be your friends. You must know how to tackle them. If you just jump in [too quickly] … they'll just ignore you. Once you have the opportunity to approach them after some [casual] talking, when they come closer you, that's the chance for you to talk. … I want them to know this is my culture, this is what Singaporeans can do. If they interested, … they become your friend. They start to learn about your culture, about everything, and then they start asking you questions.

She also shared that she often takes it upon herself to intercede when the elderly residents treat her foreign colleagues badly:

> Singaporeans, when they see foreigners they always think you're small people. If this happens in front of me, I will talk to the residents [and say], "It should not be this way. Because without them ah, how many Singaporeans [are] willing to work this kind of work, and who are skilled [and tough] enough to do this work?"

At one level, Rosnah's description of how to "do" care with foreign colleagues exemplifies the four moral dimensions of care as practice as described by Tronto (1993, 2001): attentiveness to needs ("watch and see", "if this happens in front of me"), responsibility to marshall resources to meet needs ("find time … [to] make them understand", "I will talk to the residents"), have sufficient competence ("know how to tackle them") and responsiveness ("when they come closer to you, that's the chance for you to talk"). Rosnah recognized that some are less open-minded ("because [of] different cultures [and] maybe males and females react differently"), but when they do respond, one should attempt to "learn more about them" as individuals (such as their food preferences, "these kind of things"). Yet, on another level, there are limits to unsettling the local-foreigner power hierarchy in this case. As a member of the host society, Rosnah sees herself as the one responsible for initiating contact but expects the foreigners to learn about and adapt to Singapore culture. While speaking up for her foreign co-workers demonstrates how she cares about and cares for their emotional well-being, it again indicates the power she feels she has compared to them despite claiming that she is "just a nursing aide who really can't do very much".

The same can be said of Shelley-Mae's (enrolled nurse, Philippines, female) account, despite the positive outcome. Overwhelmed by the work expected of her when she first arrived in Singapore (28 months before the interview) as a nursing aide, she cried herself to sleep every night for the first week. She "didn't know anybody … [and] ate alone". She shared how fortunate it was that her supervisor, a Singaporean, was attentive to her needs ("She saw that I was very unhappy and asked me what's wrong"), and took responsibility to comfort her ("She told me that everything is fine and I have been here only for a short while, that's why I am like that") and meet her needs ("She told two Filipino nurses to take care of me and guide me in my work"). However, although the supervisor exercised various dimensions of care ethics with Shelley-Mae, she ultimately devolved the latter's day-to-day care to foreign junior colleagues.

Arguably, limited dismantling of asymmetrical power relations also characterized care relations that workers claimed as being familial-like. For example, Singaporean Theresa's (staff nurse, female) maintained that despite the "very big difference" between locals and foreigners, the way to "bridge the gap" is to make the workers feel like family. She proudly shared that all the foreign workers in her nursing home embrace her as a mother figure ("they all call me mummy; everyone calls me mummy") because she does not get easily angered and is patient in teaching them. This family discourse appears to be another area in which the workers' paid care work with residents spills over into their relationships with colleagues. Indeed, many care workers (particularly the foreign workers) position themselves as family members rather than workers vis-à-vis their elderly charges (referring to them as "Ah Pa, Ah Ma" or "grandparents"). Yet such claims of family-like ties do not really reposition power hierarchies; the workers' continued "junior" status is reflected in the use of (grand)parental terms to refer to their local elderly residents and colleagues and some (implicit) fear of a work-mother's wrath should they make a mistake. Hence, we argue that familial terms when used among colleagues positioned differently in the formal care hierarchy do not necessarily fully undo cultural boundaries.

"Failed" unmakings?

When openness and the willingness to engage in intercultural learning about care are absent, even limited remaking of care relations may be elusive. For example, Aung (nursing aide, Myanmar, female) refrained from speaking up when her "very messy" Indian and Filipino roommates left their belongings everywhere. She decided it would be best to "just give and take" rather than confront them. She justified it by positioning herself as someone who was long-suffering and sensitive to cultural differences: "Maybe it's their culture. It's very insensitive to tell them it's wrong". By avoiding conflict, however, nothing was resolved for her and her frustration was palpable in her interview. However, as Wilson (2011, 639) notes, "While overlooked codes of conduct might produce nothing more than slight irritation", they could also "initiate a much more charged or disruptive response or avowal". Indeed, in cases where intercultural learning breaks down, emotional ruptures can occur. Wei (nursing aide, PRC, female) recounted a Chinese colleague's experience of sharing a room with a Filipino:

> She told me that the Filipino is very messy and she is a person who is very particular about cleanliness. She wanted the Filipino to be tidier but the Filipino insisted that it's her own area and she could do whatever she wanted. They had a few arguments. ... So the China healthcare worker requested for a change of room.

Although these cases could be interpreted as examples of failed moments of intercultural encounter, it is also possible to think about responses to difficult situations as struggles to recognize colleagues' subjective positions while acting in ways to prevent further problems. Perhaps, as Halberstam (2011, 3) has argued, rather than being understood as the inability to comply with social norms, "failure" may be seen as a means of unveiling "more cooperative ways ... of being in the world", thereby disrupting its clean boundary with success. In other words, meaningful encounters are not just about the immediate production of positive feelings and outcomes. A multicultural ethics of care approach sensitizes us to the multiple ways emotions, ranging from the negative to the positive, are sites for (un)learning about (reciprocal) care, moving one from "detached observer" to "involved performer" because of increased "emotional involvement" and a better "grasp of social meaning" over time (Bowden 1997, 108). The processual, relational and dynamic approach of a multicultural care ethic facilitates recognition that feelings and encounters are embedded in ongoing interactions and evolving relationships with the potential for change. As Raghuram (2019, 19, citing

Okano 2016) succinctly observes, "'the ethic of care does not teach us how to heal wounded people effectively but rather teaches us how difficult it is to do so' and its outcomes are not always guaranteed".

Conclusion

As "carework spills crosses national borders to encompass changes in the global division of labour" (Jacoby 2006, 7), there will be increased intercultural mixing in societies that demand and receive migrant care workers. Much of this mixing takes place in mundane spaces such as cafes, local parks, hospitals and nursing homes. According to Wilson (2017, 457), "the potential that encounters [between people of different cultures] pose for learning and politics" makes them "compelling as a site of analysis". By adopting Joan Tronto's care ethic to examine the routine intercultural interactions that take place among culturally-, nationally- and ethnically- diverse healthcare workers in nursing homes in Singapore, we gained insight into the specific practices and processes used to negotiate their cultural boundaries and move towards intercultural mixing and multicultural learning.

While the workers make deliberate decisions to care about, care for, as well give and receive care to/from one another, they do not consciously practise Tronto's aspects of *ethical care*. Yet, their descriptions of intercultural mixing were characterized by the moral dimensions of attentiveness, responsibility, competence and responsiveness in their relationships with one another. Despite lines that divide, multicultural subjects who are open to the possibility of knowing cultural others, and who are willing to engage in as well as respond to ethical care even if not consciously, are able to exercise a "capacity for empathic connecting" (Green 2012, 4). Through everyday acts of care over a sustained period, they embark on pathways of possibility to progress from disconnection to mutual knowing. In her critique of the way theorisations of care ethics have been largely predicated on universalist (i.e. "western") conceptualisations of care, Raghuram (2016, 2019) has urged scholars to attend to contextually-embedded meanings and geohistories of care. This paper heeds Raghuram's call in two ways. First, by foregrounding the way Asian discourses about the "family" and its associated values (e.g. harmony, respect) are drawn upon in framing the way care should be practised. While there are variations in the way caring bodies are expected to "learn to negotiate each other and co-exist in mobile care settings" (Raghuram 2016, 5230) – and notwithstanding the fact that "family" characteristics may be fictive – the notion of treating one another as "family" is used by healthcare workers to describe valued care relationships. Second, by training our analytical lenses on care practices located in an Asian multicultural setting, we extend our understanding of the possibilities and limits underlying the idea of a "multicultural ethics of care". While Singapore-style multiculturalism is a form of multiculturalism that deepens the foreign-local divide at the structural level (in terms of legal status, conditions of stay, access to community resources and so on), it provides an environment that enables intercultural learning and respect, particularly in terms of the conduct of everyday life, if one is open to the possibility.

While a focus on the mundane reveals how connections are built and relationships established across cultural differences when there is a reciprocal willingness to engage in multicultural sociability, this paper also argues that emotional flashpoints and sustained disagreement need not be regarded as failed moments. "Failed" intercultural engagements do not necessarily signal the dismantling of care/care ethics but can also reveal the "potential to redraw and negotiate the field of what might be possible" (Wilson 2011, 645). Overcoming disappointments and differences to close the gap in multicultural learning takes time and mutual (though not necessarily equal) effort on both sides. While the outcomes are not always predictable, persistence and reciprocity allow for the possibility that a transformation of attitudes will transpire, differences will be surmounted and new ways found to "live with difference".

Notes

1. Among the various care theories, Joan Tronto's is the one most often applied to discussions of the ethics of nursing care practice, probably because of its focus on the practice of care in meeting the question "How can I best meet my caring responsibility?" See, for example, Green (2012), Lachman (2012) and Vanlaere and Gastmans (2007).
2. We are grateful to a reviewer for helping us express this idea clearly.
3. Migrant streams from China and India into colonial Singapore began in the nineteenth century, soon after its founding in 1819. The Chinese population in particular, increased rapidly and by the early twentieth century was just over 70 per cent, while the Indian population comprised about 8 per cent. These proportions have largely remained since.
4. Although limited in number, nursing homes (then known as "homes for the aged") were established by charitable organizations in Singapore as early as the 1930s. The earliest homes provided accommodation for destitute elderly immigrants. With the anticipated rise in the number of elderly arising from the baby boomers, the state provided subsidies (up to 90 per cent of capital costs for construction and 50 per cent of operating costs) to encourage the growth of nursing homes from the 1990s. This led to a growth in the number of homes, although the exact number is unknown (Wong, Yap, and Pang 2014).
5. As there are no official statistics on the distribution of healthcare workers by nationality working in Singapore's nursing homes, we do not know how representative our sample of interviewees is. While we tried to obtain employment numbers by nationality from the nursing home operators we interviewed, many chose not to share the specific distributions. The distribution in our sample reflects the overall picture painted by the operators.

6. Singlish is a colloquial form of English spoken in Singapore. Its sentence structure, vocabulary and intonation borrow primarily from the main Chinese dialects spoken in Singapore and to a lesser extent, from Malay and Tamil (mainly spoken by the Malays and Indians).

Disclosure statement

No potential conflict of interest was reported by the authors.

Funding

This work was supported by National University of Singapore and Japan Society for the Promotion of Science: [Grant Number JSPS/JRP/06/FASS1].

ORCID

Shirlena Huang 🆔 http://orcid.org/0000-0001-8932-6362
Brenda S.A. Yeoh 🆔 http://orcid.org/0000-0002-0240-3175

References

Allport, G. W. 1954. *The Nature of Prejudice*. Reading, MA: Addison-Wesley.
Amin, A. 2002. "Ethnicity and the Multicultural City: Living with Diversity." *Environment and Planning A: Economy and Space* 34 (6): 959–980.
Askins, K. 2015. "Being Together: Everyday Geographies and the Quiet Politics of Belonging." *ACME* 14 (2): 470–478.
Bowden, P. 1997. *Caring: Gender-Sensitive Ethics*. London & New York: Routledge.
Clayton, J. 2009. "Thinking Spatially: Towards an Everyday Understanding of Inter-Ethnic Relations." *Social & Cultural Geography* 10 (4): 481–498.
Department of Statistics, Singapore. 2017. *Population Trends 2017*. Singapore: Department of Statistics, Ministry of Trade and Industry.
Featherstone, B., and K. Morris. 2012. "Feminist Ethics of Care." In *The SAGE Handbook of Social Work*, edited by M. Gray, J. Midgley, and S. A. Webb, 341–354. London: Sage.
Frisina, A. 2012. "Multiculturalism." In *Encyclopedia of Global Religion*, edited by M. Juergensmeyer, and W. C. Roof, 837–840. Thousand Oaks: Sage.
Green, B. 2012. "Applying Feminist Ethics of Care to Nursing Practice." *Journal of Nursing and Care* 1 (3). doi:10.4172/2167-1168.1000111.
Halberstam, J. J. 2011. *The Queer Art of Failure*. Durham: Duke University Press.
Hankivsky, O. 2014. "Rethinking Care Ethics: On the Promise and Potential of an Intersectional Analysis." *American Political Science Review* 108 (2): 252–264.
Hardy, S. 2014. *What's White about Multiculturalism? Exploring Everyday Multiculturalism, Prejudice and Targeted Hostility with Young White British People in Leicester*, Thesis Submitted for the Degree of Doctor of Philosophy, Department of Criminology, University of Leicester, UK.
Ho, E. L. E. 2019. *Citizens in Motion: Emigration, Immigration, and Re-migration across China's Borders*. Stanford: Stanford California Press.
Huang, S., B. S. A. Yeoh, and M. Toyota. 2012. "Caring for the Elderly: The Embodied Labour of Migrant Care Workers in Singapore." *Global Networks* 12 (2): 195–215.

Jacobs, J. M. 1996. *Edge of Empire: Postcolonialism and the City*. London: Routledge.

Jacoby, D. 2006. "Caring about Caring Labour: An Introduction." *Politics & Society* 34 (1): 5–10.

Lachman, V. D. 2012. "Applying the Ethics of Care to Your Nursing Practice." *Medsurg Nursing* 21 (2): 112–116.

Leung, T., and S. Menon. 2011. "Who Will Look after Our Elderly?" *TODAY* (Singapore), 13 June.

Ministry of Manpower. 2018. Foreign Workforce Numbers. http://www.mom.gov.sg/documents-and-publications/foreign-workforce-numbers.

Neal, S., and C. Vincent. 2013. "Multiculture, Middle Class Competencies and Friendship Practices in Super-Diverse Geographies." *Social & Cultural Geography* 14 (8): 909–929.

Radford, D. 2016. "'Everyday Otherness' – Intercultural Refugee Encounters and Everyday Multiculturalism in a South Australian Rural Town." *Journal of Ethnic and Migration Studies* 42 (3): 2128–2145.

Raghuram, P. 2016. "Locating Care Ethics beyond the Global North." *ACME: An International Journal for Critical Geographies* 15 (3): 511–533.

Raghuram, P. 2019. "Race and Feminist Care Ethics: Intersectionality as Method." *Gender, Place & Culture*. doi:10.1080/0966369X.2019.1567471.

Ramdas, K. 2016. "Feminist Care Ethics, Becoming Area." *Environment and Planning D: Society and Space* 34 (5): 843–849.

Scuzzarello, S. 2015. "Caring Multiculturalism: Power and Transformation in Diverse Societies." *Feminist Theory* 16 (1): 67–86.

Siddique, S. 1989. "Singapore Identity." In *Management of Success: The Moulding of Modern Singapore*, edited by K. S. Sandhu, and P. Wheatley, 563–577. Singapore: Institute of Southeast Asian Studies.

Tronto, J. C. 1993. *Moral Boundaries: A Political Argument for an Ethic of Care*. New York: Routledge.

Tronto, J. C. 2001. "An Ethic of Care." In *Ethics in Community-Based Eldercare*, edited by M. Holstein, and P. B. Mitzen, 60–68. New York: Springer.

Uitermark, J., U. Rossi, and H. van Houtum. 2005. "Reinventing Multiculturalism: Urban Citizenship and the Negotiation of Ethnic Diversity in Amsterdam." *International Journal of Urban and Regional Research* 29 (3): 622–640.

Valentine, G. 2008. "Living with Difference: Reflections on Geographies of Encounter." *Progress in Human Geography* 32 (3): 323–337.

Vanlaere, L., and C. Gastmans. 2007. "Ethics in Nursing Education: Learning to Reflect on Care Practices." *Nursing Ethics* 14 (6): 758–766.

Vertovec, S. 2007. "Super-Diversity and its Implications." *Ethnic and Racial Studies* 30 (6): 1024–1054.

Wilson, H. F. 2011. "Passing Propinquities in the Multicultural City: The Everyday Encounters of Bus Passengering." *Environment and Planning A: Economy and Space* 43 (3): 634–649.

Wilson, H. F. 2017. "On Geography and Encounter: Bodies, Borders, and Difference." *Progress in Human Geography* 41 (4): 451–471.

Wise, A. 2014. "Everyday Multiculturalism." In *Migration: A COMPAS Anthology*, edited by B. Anderson, and M. Keith. Oxford: COMPAS. http://compasanthology.co.uk/wp-content/uploads/2014/02/Wise_COMPASMigrationAnthology.pdf.

Wong, G. H. Z., P. L. K. Yap, and W. S. Pang. 2014. "Changing Landscape of Nursing Homes in Singapore: Challenges in the 21st Century." *Annals, Academy of Medicine* 43 (1): 44–50.

Yantzi, N. M., and M. W. Skinner. 2009. "Care/Caregiving." In *International Encyclopedia of Human Geography (Social and Cultural Geography)*, edited by R. Kitchin, and N. Thrift, 402–407. Oxford: Elsevier.

Ye, J. 2017. "Managing Urban Diversity through Differential Inclusion in Singapore." *Environment and Planning D: Society and Space* 35 (6): 1033–1052.

Iphones and "African gangs": everyday racism and ethno-transnational media in Melbourne's Chinese student world

Fran Martin ⓘ

ABSTRACT

Based on an ethnography of young women from China studying in Melbourne, this article explores participants' experiences of living in a super-diverse city, and questions whether extant theoretical accounts of everyday multiculturalism are adequate to understand the experience of these residents. In 2016, Melbourne's Chinese student community was rocked by a prolonged spate of mobile phone thefts that Chinese-language social media framed as ethnically targeted attacks on Chinese people by "African gangs." This article considers participants' responses to these incidents, alongside the racialized reportage of them on the WeChat public accounts that are participants' main source of local news. The article mounts a critique of the media ethics inherent in this form of news delivery. It extends the everyday multiculturalism framework with an example that deals not with a strongly hybrid migrant youth culture, but rather with young migrants socialized into a monocultural society encountering everyday life in super-diversity.

In May 2016, an anonymous poster (Figure 1) was attached to a post near the building entrance in inner-northern Melbourne used by the Trinity College Foundation Studies Program, a bridging programme to tertiary study for inter-natinoal students, including many from China. With its simplified-character Chinese text reading "Danger. African criminals" accompanied by photo-graphs of hostile-looking African-heritage young men, and assertions that such men target Chinese students to "rob" and "bash" them, the above photo-graph of the poster was circulated among Chinese international students via WeChat, currently the most popular social media platform in this community. It fed into a stream of posts and news stories that had been running since Feb-ruary concerning the alleged targeting of Chinese students by "African gangs"

Figure 1. Poster on Swanston St Melbourne, May 9 2016.

in a spate of iPhone thefts in the area. In light of its obvious racial vilification, accusation of unidentified people, and doubt cast on the efficacy of the authorities, unsurprisingly, the poster was swiftly removed by police.

This poster points toward hostile engagements (allegedly physical, definitely rhetorical) between two racialized groups within inner Melbourne's urban multiculture: "African migrants" and "Chinese international students". In pitting these groups agains each other, the poster highlights class as well as "racial" differences. While African-heritage youth in Melbourne may be the children of former refugees from Sudan, South Sudan, and the Horn of Africa – among the city's most severely disadvantaged residents on multiple socio-economic indicators (Olliff and Mohamed 2007; Dhanji 2009; Gatt 2011; Abur 2012) – the many Chinese international students studying in the city come mainly from middle-class and elite families in urban China, where tertiary education in a "developed" western country has become a desirable commodity to increase competitiveness in China's professional job market (Martin 2017b). What is happening here? What led to this poster being produced, displayed, and circulated? Are our current interpretative frame-works adequate for the task of accounting for it, or making scholarly interven-tions into the situation that produces it? This article attempts to tackle these questions.

I begin, below, by revisiting the frameworks of everyday multiculturalism and everyday racism. I then offer a brief consideration of racial discourses in contemporary China, where the international student participants in the eth-nographic study on which this article is based grew up and were socialized. This is followed by a detailed analysis of the phone thefts case study, including critical consideration of the role of new transnational social media in shaping Chinese students' experiences of race and urban life in Melbourne. The paper concludes with a consideration of the implications of this example for our understandings of everyday multiculturalism in the context of super-diversity.

Revisiting everyday multiculturalism and everyday racism

Since the late 1990s, a thread of critical work from scholars in Australia and Britain has problematized the top-down accounts of "official multiculturalism" prescribed by governments through attention to people's material practices of living with cultural diversity "on the ground," in a turn toward what has been called "everyday multiculturalism." In Jon Stratton's germinal account in *Race Daze*, he introduces the concept as referring to:

> how cultures, produced by individuals in their everyday lives, merge, creolise and transform as people live their lives, adapting to and resisting situations, and (mis)understanding, loving, hating and taking pleasure in other people with whom they come into contact. (Stratton 1998, 15)

In Australia, scholars have taken up this rubric to produce enriched under-standings of the unspectacular daily business of living in diversity, in a cultural climate where multiculturalism has come under renewed attack from the (re)emergence of Hansonism, Islamophobia, and moral panics about "ethnic gangs" (Ang et al. 2002; Wise 2005; Stratton 2006; Bloch and Dreher 2009; Wise and Velayutham 2009a; Colic-Peisker and Farquharson 2011; Collins, Reid, and Fabiansson 2011; Ho 2011; Wise 2011; Harris 2013).

An important corollary to this work is a related strand of work by some of the same scholars on everyday racism (Stratton 2006; Bloch and Dreher 2009). Drawing on the earlier work of Essed (1991), Stratton frames this as:

> the day-to-day, common-sense ideological legitimations that [...] people [...] developed to justify their racist practices [... ;] the formation of attitudes and understandings that are so embedded in the everyday life of a racialized culture [...] that members of that culture [...] don't even recognize themselves as making decisions based in a racialized history. (Stratton 2006, 662)

Everyday racism is at root what this article is about. However, it departs from the classic works in everyday multiculturalism studies in its focus on recently-arrived migrants; on the impact of transnational flows on local-level inter-group relations; and on how racial and class hierarchies in a super-diverse society fuel everyday racism *between* ethnic groups. Many studies of inter-national students and racism in Australia have tended to frame these students exclusively as victims of racist violence from the majority culture (e.g. Dunn, Pelleri, and Maeder-Han 2011). This paper shows that international students are not *only* victims of racism in Australia (although they certainly are that), but also are embedded into complex, transnational racialized hierarchies, and may themselves be complicit in racisms that morph and evolve along with educational mobility.

Referencing Vertovec's (2007) conceptualization of "super-diversity" in Britain, Greg Noble characterizes everyday life in Australian cities with refer-ence to a related kind of "diversification of diversity":

> Australia seems to be evincing an evolving "hyper-diversity": it wasn't just that people lived hybrid lives, or lived them in polyethnic neighbourhoods, but that complexity and its subsequent forms of interaction were of such a nature that they went beyond typical understandings of multiculturalism and corre-sponded to the claim that diversity was becoming more diverse. (Noble 2009, 47)

I wish to underline two elements in this formulation, both because they characterize much recent work on everyday multiculturalism in Australia, and because the case study I address here presents a potential challenge to each of them,which suggests that it may now be useful to extend earlier work on everyday multiculturalism in order to take account of changing social conditions. First, as a precondition for the emergence of hyper-diversity, Noble cites the concept of *hybrid lives*. This concept of hybridity appears often in the work of Australian scholars in their collective emphasis on culturally and ethnically mixed cultures among 1.5- and second- and third-generation migrant youth (e.g. Ang et al. 2002; Wise and Velayutham 2009b, 6; Collins, Reid, and Fabiansson 2011; Harris 2013). Second, Noble's formulation cites the *polyethnic neighbourhood* as another precondition for Australian hyper-diversity, and a key site for research on everyday multiculturalism. Much work on everyday multiculturalism in Australia has focused on territorially bounded sites relating to local communities: specific neighbourhoods (Bloch and Dreher 2009; Wise 2009, 2005; Collins, Reid, and Fabiansson 2011; Harris 2013); schools (Ho 2011); community organizations (Wise 2011), and so on.

Although the extant scholarship's focus on hybrid identities and specific localities certainly identifies productive sites for research on everyday multi-culturalism, to do justice to the conditions of social life in cities like Melbourne today, I argue that we need to go further. First, I propose that *we should supplement attention to hybrid identities among permanent migrants with studies of interactions involving more recently arrived first-generation and transient migrants.* Although doubtless, for most migrants, degrees of subjective hybridization develop over time in a non-linear way; nevertheless, as a result of the shorter length of time they have spent in Australia, recently arrived first-generation and temporary migrants are likely to experience their own ethno-cultural identities in significantly different ways from the 1.5+ generations who have been the main focus of the studies cited above. This is certainly the case in the present study, in which the vast majority of participants, when questioned about their ethno-cultural identification, continue to describe themselves as Chinese nationals (*Zhongguoren*: a term that implies citizenship of the People's Republic of China as well as Chinese racial-cultural identity) first and foremost. One of the key points in Vertovec's original conceptualization of super-diversity is the diversification of migration statuses, with permanent migrants living alongside transient migrants like students and guest workers, and ever-renewing waves of first-generation arrivals (Vertovec 2007). Thus, even while 1.5+ migrant generations undeniably do mix, hybridize, and render problematic the concept of discrete, ethno-bounded cultures, this hybridization is not universal or even across all groups in super-diverse societies. Rather, we see the co-existence of multiple migrant generations, including relatively recently arrived first-generation and transient migrants, some of whom may not have time to mix and hybridize to the same extent as permanent migrants and their succeeding generations and may in fact believe rather strongly in the existence and importance of "categorical ethnic definitions" (Harris 2013, 22). If the point of theorizations of everyday multiculturalism is to develop an understanding of how social life actually works under conditions of diversity, then we must take into account the experiences of the full range of groups that make up that diversity. Under current conditions in the large east coast Australian cities, recent and transient migrants like international students are a group that should not be ignored.

Second, I propose that *we should supplement existing conceptualizations of multiculturalism with a stronger appreciation of the transnational character of people's everyday experience.* The extant everyday multiculturalism scholarship's emphasis on territorially bounded places at times risks the implication that "everydayness" equates to the geographic scale of the locality. Yet today – perhaps especially for migrant communities – the terrain of everyday life is often strongly translocal as much as geo-local, so that to think about everyday multiculturalism is, ipso facto, to think about translocality (Amin 2002a; Vertovec 2007, 1043; Harris 2013, 110–117). Thanks to the quasi-ubiquity of broadband connectivity, the ready availability of mobile communication technologies, the naturalization of online digital communication in everyday life, and the decreased costs of international travel, for the current generations of migrant young people in Australian cities, everyday life is thoroughly shot through with translocal connections (Smith 2001; Martin and Rizvi 2014). For a study like this one, in which the research subject group is intensively net-worked through media and personal connections to people, texts, and cultures located at a transnational remove from the context of their immediate habitation in Melbourne, I find a translocal approach extremely useful. It enables us to see "the everyday [...] not as a sedentary, nostalgic site of 'local culture,' but as a dynamic crossroads of local, national, and transnational place-making practices" (Smith 2001, 185) in ways that do justice to the actual conditions of many people's experiences of everyday life in super-diverse societies.

The material presented in this article is drawn from a five-year longitudinal ethnographic study still in progress at the time of writing, in which I am fol-lowing a group of 56 female tertiary students from pre-departure from China through several years of study in Australia, and on to their post-gradu-ation destinations. The purpose of this study is to develop an in-depth under-standing of the social and subjective world of this group of students, including their everyday experiences of living with cultural diversity in Australian cities. In this article, I draw on several data sources, including: discussions with par-ticipants, their families, future international students, and commercial inter-national education agents in China during June–July 2015; a series of ongoing informal conversations and formal recorded interviews with partici-pants between July 2015 and October 2018 (both face-to-face and via social media) in which they discuss their everyday experiences in Melbourne; 39 months' informal daily observations of participants' activity on WeChat includ-ing the content of the links they shared to local news stories on WeChat public accounts; and my discussions with a number of other informants, including other members of Melbourne's Chinese diasporic community, people involved at various levels in the production of WeChat local news media, and representatives of Victoria Police, the University of Melbourne, and com-munity groups providing services to refugees and multicultural youth in Melbourne.

Race and Africanness in modern Chinese public culture

Before turning to the racialized panic that is this article's main case study, it is necessary first to briefly survey constructions of race (*zhongzu*), and especially of African racial identity, in modern and contemporary China. This complex topic has been treated in depth by a number of major studies (for example Dikötter 1992; Johnson 2007), but a key point to highlight in this brief summary is the lengthy cultural shadow cast by the Chinese adaptation of European scientific racism in the early twentieth century. As Frank Dikötter demonstrates, the Chinese discourse of race that took shape in that period took on aspects of racial biologism, evolutionism and eugenics to (re)produce a racial hierarchy with northern European and Han races at the top and darker-skinned peoples, especially Africans, at the bottom (Dikötter 1992, 61–190). Africans as a "race" were associated in China's Republican era public culture with barbarism, backwardness (*luohou*), uncivility and intellectual inferiority.

The discourse of race was officially abolished with the founding of the People's Republic in 1949. But in a functionally mono-ethnic society with no strong social pressures to develop anti-racist critique, and where national belonging has long been conceptualized in racialized terms, the earlier racist discourse on hierarchized differences between the world's ethnic groups has continued clearly and persistently to shape popular attitudes, through the Maoist era and into the present (Dikötter 1992, 191–195). This can be seen in outbreaks of hostility toward African students on Chinese university campuses during the 1980s, with the Africans stereotyped as uncultured, uncivilized, hypersexualized and sexually predatory (Cheng 2011). A related discourse surfaces in outbursts of anti-African racism online in the contemporary era of increased China-Africa aid, trade, and human mobility (Cheng 2011; Pfafman, Carpenter, and Tang 2015).

Modern Chinese anti-African racism clearly resonates with racist discourses globally (Pfafman, Carpenter, and Tang 2015). In particular, aspects of the representational patterns outlined above echo those found in contemporary Australian public culture, where moral panics over "Sudanese refugees" have become a media staple over the past decade. News reports persistently represent African-heritage youth in Australian cities as a racially othered "problem group" associated with urban decay, violence, delinquency and gang-related crime (Windle 2008; Nolan et al. 2011; Abur 2012). In the events of 2016 in Melbourne's central city area, I suggest, Chinese and Australian (and global) racist frames for interpreting young African-heritage men's presence in the city came together and became mutually amplified.

Phones, gangs, and WeChat

However, despite common stereotypes that construct Chinese international students as insular and not amenable to intra-cultural mixing and exchange, in fact, Australia's multicultural society is one of the nation's major draw-cards as a study destination for these students. In the pre-departure information sessions I attended in 2015 in China, run by Australian universities and commercial education agents, Australia's multiculturalism was regularly cited in the standard list of attractions of the country, both by education industry professionals and by future students and their parents. Specifically, agents led prospective students and their parents to believe that racism would not affect them in Australia, since it was a land of multicultural harmony. Emphasis was placed more on multiculturalism as a safeguard against anti-Chinese racism specifically than on the intrinsic value of multicultural mixing among a variety of ethnic groups. But the vast majority of my future-student intervie-wees did express the hope of broadening their horizons by making friends across cultures while studying in Australia. While most expressed the specific hope to befriend "local" (*dangdi*, which in their habitual usage usually means "white": Martin 2017a)[1] peers, one future student who intro-duced herself to me at a university-run pre-departure session said she was especially interested in participating in my study since, as an undergraduate, she herself had conducted a study into the everyday experience of African international students on her campus in Hangzhou.

Following their arrival in Melbourne, while many of my participants have found it difficult to make "local" friends, some have developed friendships and romantic relationships with other east and southeast Asian international students, including people from Taiwan, Japan, Malaysia, Thailand, Vietnam, Indonesia and India. One young woman, finding herself one of just two Chinese students in her course at a campus in Melbourne's outer north, devel-oped close friendships with a group of Muslim women students: one from Syria, one from Turkey, and an Anglo-Celtic Australian woman who is married to a Muslim man and has converted to Islam. "I often look around and find that I'm the only one not wearing a head scarf!" she joked, seemingly surprised (pleasantly) by this unexpected turn in the ethno-cultural compo-sition of her friendship group. She told me how she enjoyed learning about her Muslim friends' religion and cultural traditions, and admires their studious-ness and ambition. Another participant, already a resident in Melbourne for several years, had a romantic relationship with an international postgraduate student from Ghana (which she did not mention to her parents, as she foresaw they would object to her dating somebody African). Another, more recently arrived and currently enrolled in an English-language class, spoke forthrightly about how her experience of the multicultural classroom and new friendships with Saudi and Indian classmates have changed her former view of certain nationalities, which was influenced by negative discourse from the Chinese state, based largely on current political disputes. Thus not only is multiculturalism a significant draw-card for Chinese students coming to study in Australia, but once they are here, many of them make significant cross-cultural engagements and, as a result, develop varying levels of reflex-ivity regarding national and cultural identity (Martin 2016). Nonetheless, it is notable that in these engagements, while students may cross lines of ethni-city, culture and "race," class lines remain fairly intact, since their socializing habits tend to remain within the orbit of the campus and international student groups in particular.

It was in fact through a reflexive critical engagement with questions of ethnicity and media representation that I first became aware of the unfolding events that constitute my central case study. In early March 2016, at one of my project's regular group activities (an evening film screening), Niuniu, a 24 year-old Masters student from central China, addressed the group: "You know all these stories on WeChat lately, about African gangs attacking Chinese students? Well, I'm wondering whether they're really true, or whether they could be a media beat-up." Niuniu described how she had followed up on a number of stories currently circulating and contacted anyone she could who was connected with the stories, only to find that she couldn't locate any direct eye-witnesses or victims of the reported attacks. She therefore suspected it was a media beat-up, harmful both to inter-ethnic relations and to Chinese students' sense of safety. Other participants were less reflexive and skeptical, simply fearing for their own safety – especially since some WeChat news accounts linked reader reports of muggings with the story of a recent "home invasion" and carjacking by an "African gang" in the Eastern suburbs.

Over the following days, stories of Chinese students being mugged in the university environs by groups of "tall, fast, black youths" came in thick and fast on WeChat – both in our dedicated chat group for study participants, and via WeChat's Facebook-like "Moments" feed, where I had around 250 contacts in the wider Chinese student community. A sense of panic set in, with many students stating that they dare not go out alone or at night in the Carlton/ city area, and some reporting that people they knew directly had been robbed, and had underwhelming experiences with reporting thefts to the police, who appeared to "do nothing." This culminated on the night of March 12, when a violent disturbance took place in Federation Square during Moomba celebrations (Melbourne's annual city festival), which was widely reported in local media as involving rival "African" and "Pacific Islander" gangs from Melbourne's disadvantaged outer east (Smith 2016). WeChat Melbourne news accounts picked up the sensationalist stories from the local tabloid press, translated the headlines into Chinese and in many cases exacerbated the racist cast of the reporting, adding photos of injuries sustained by ethnically Chinese people, and referring repeatedly to "black gang members" and "black bandits" "out of control" and targeting "Asians" (*yayi*) or "Chinese people" (*Huaren*). Chinese student groups encouraged their members to contact the Chinese Consulate in Melbourne to voice concern over whether the police and university were adequately safeguarding their security. Students' families back in China, where stories of the allegedly anti-Chinese crimes in Melbourne circulated freely via online and social media, sent panicked messages. Meanwhile Victoria Police attempted – somewhat ineffectually, given their lack of access to Chinese-language media – to circulate a de-racializing message that the muggings were not targeted at Chinese people specifically, and only one-third of phone theft victims were of Asian heritage (Worrall 2016).

In my discussions with participants over the weeks and months that followed, it was clear that their levels of fear and insecurity in the city and university area had significantly increased as a result of their consumption of WeChat stories about the activities of the "black gang members" supposedly "targeting Chinese students." Many reported now feeling generically afraid of "black people" and unwilling to encounter them in the street.

The reports that students were reading via WeChat came not only from their personal Moments feed (*pengyou quan*), where users interact directly with friends, but also from their subscription to local news accounts (*gongzhong hao*). Usually, these are produced by commercial companies, and offer a daily digest of Chinese-language news and information about life and events in specific Australian cities. The subscription accounts and individuals' personal WeChat communications exist in a symbiotic relationship. While individuals often post links to stories published in the official accounts, the official accounts in turn rely on user-produced content as a source of stories, presenting screen shots of users' posts or messages as eyewitness accounts of unfolding events. The content of MelToday is organically linked, too, with local Australian media, with a preference for eye-grabbing material gleaned from publications from Rupert Murdoch's News Corp empire and other tabloid media.

Subscription accounts of this type occupy a unique emerging place in both local and transnational media ecologies. WeChat is a Chinese-owned and -run service, developed by China's Tencent Holdings Ltd and regulated almost wholly from the Chinese side. State censorship of content applies, so that even when operating in Australia, content producers self-censor to avoid criticism of China's government and the Chinese Communist Party. On the Australian side, however, these public subscription services tend to be somewhat insulated from Australian Commonwealth media regulation – for example, the enforcement of anti-racial vilification laws, political campaigning laws, and so on – due to the language barrier to Australian authorities. In terms of content, though, accounts like MelToday, Melbourne WeLife and Mel_life – three of my participants' most commonly read accounts – present news and information that is almost wholly concerned with local current events in Melbourne. In this sense, WeChat news subscription accounts occupy an emergent grey area between traditional "ethnic" media and new forms of transnational media; hence I dub them "ethno-transnational media." Like the "ethno-specific mediatized sphericules" analyzed by Stuart Cunningham a decade and a half ago – at that time instantiated in video, television, cinema, music, and Web 1.0 platforms used by diasporic communities in Australia – these new media, too, are probably *most* significant insofar as they provide users with sorely needed spaces of intra-diasporic communication, social support, and a minoritarian public sphere (Cunningham 2001; Martin and Rizvi 2014). However, the new generation of social media services also has a number of new characteristics that, as we will see, arguably make its social effects more complex than the older media analysed by Cunningham.

The importance of WeChat in Chinese international students' everyday lives cannot be overstated. Most of my participants keep the app open on their phones 24 h a day, and check their Moments feed and subscription accounts multiple times, and for cumulatively significant periods of time, every day and night. Their preference for sourcing aggregated news via mobile apps reflects a general global trend (Bell 2016; Tang 2016; Taylor 2016). In China, a recent study by Tencent shows that WeChat is among people's top sources for accessing news, especially via WeChat's official accounts service (WalkTheChat 2016). Travelling abroad for study, Chinese students continue to practice these news-sourcing habits learned at home.

Each of the Melbourne-based official accounts to which my research participants and I subscribe covered the incidents outlined above to some extent. While some made an effort to disentangle fact from fiction, one account stands out for its extensive and sensationalist coverage of "African gangs" stories both before the Moomba events and since. MelToday (*Jinri Moerben*, web version available at: http://www.meltoday.com) is among the largest and most widely read of the Melbourne-based accounts, operating across Weibo, WeChat, its own webpage, and a dedicated phone app. Its top WeChat headline stories attract between 10,000 and 100,000 views; around 35,000 views at a rough average (for context, currently around 50,000 students from China are studying in Victoria; Herbert 2016). In 2015, MelToday reported that it had over 150,000 followers on Weibo, over 50,000 on WeChat with 7,000–8,000 ongoing monthly growth, and over 1 million monthly views from 250,000 unique visitors to its webpage (Jinri Chuanmei Jituan 2015, 18; 21). MelToday, registered as a share limited company in 2014, is part of the Media Today Group founded and directed by young entrepreneur Dapeng "Roc" Zhang, a graduate of the University of Technology Sydney (UTS), following his establishment of the similar SydneyToday service in 2010. MelToday, a successful commercial enterprise employing 10 staff, including five reporters, uses tabloid-style headlines and images soliciting attention-grabbing emotional responses – shock, astonishment, fear, outrage, (Chinese) patriotism, pathos, intrigue, and so on – to draw readers in to click on stories on a range of topics deemed to be of interest to the Chinese community, especially immigration, investment, real estate, education, entertainment, and crime.

In mid-2016, I met with one of the partners in MelToday, Mr A. – a young finance graduate from an Australian university – and spoke with him about the company's approach to news reporting. Young people today, he explained, want news fast, conveniently, cheaply, and in few words; and

Chinese people prefer it in Chinese. And they need news media that will represent issues of particular concern for Chinese people (*Huaren*), to which the local media do not give a lot of attention. Mr A. told me that whereas traditional news's higher budget gives it the advantage of in-depth reporting and systematic fact checking, the advantage of social media news lies in its speed. MelToday's fact checking is minimal, often confined to a simple Internet search to ascertain whether reported events actually occurred. Its editors choose news topics based on an evaluation of their likely popularity: the goal is to keep up traffic to the account since the operational model is wholly commercial, relying on the sale of space, whose value is based on traffic volume, to advertisers. Echoing other WeChat news account workers I have spoken with, Mr A. observed candidly that to keep the traffic up, writers routinely take stories from the local press and "just, you know, exaggerate things a *little* bit, for the headline." As well as this commercially driven sensationalism, Mel-Today's copy is also marked by its insistent use of the term "Chinese people" (*Huaren*: a term that indicates Chinese ethnic or racial identity as well as cultural affiliation), constructing *Huaren* heroes, *Huaren* crime victims, *Huaren* concerns, and *Huaren* responses to current affairs, thus continually reinforcing "Chinese" ethnic identity as both the lynchpin of reader engagement and the lens through which local events are evaluated.

It was very clear from our conversation that Mr A.'s first priority was profit: delivering news content with high clickability to guarantee advertising revenue. Of course, this is not idiosyncratic, but part of a broader trend toward the tabloidization and "infotainment-ization" of journalism in deregulating, commercial digital media environments the world over (Bennett 2004; Fenton 2010). Here, however, we see a new permutation of this trend: sensationalized local news delivered through a highly popular form of commercial ethno-transnational media that is somewhat insulated from content regulation in the jurisdiction where it operates – with concrete ramifications for that city's multicultural livability. This particular example of ethno-transnational tabloid news media tends to reinforce categorical ethnic definitions, encouraging readers to understand themselves as part of, and loyal to, a specific and rather non-hybrid group (*Huaren*), understood *in distinction and often opposition to* other groups including "refugees" and "Africans."

As noted above, overall I observed that continued exposure to sensationalist reporting on "African gangs" by MelToday and other WeChat local news accounts tended to have the net effect of increasing Chinese students' mistrust of people they thought were African, and eroding their sense of safety in the public spaces of the city. Nevertheless, if we examine their responses to these events in greater depth, a more complex picture emerges. Many participants revealed a high degree of reflexivity in their consumption of media like MelToday: it is known among readers as a deeply sensationalist platform, and many – as we saw above with Niuniu – tend to approach its stories with significant skepticism. A couple of months after the main wave of reports on phone thefts, one participant, Jiale (18), took a very calm, pragmatic approach to the issue, observing that in big cities like Guangzhou – her hometown – such thefts occur all the time and yet are seldom reported (indeed, over the course of this study quite a few participants have returned from trips back to China reporting quite blandly that their phones were stolen while they were there). In Melbourne, by contrast, Jiale thought that because the Chinese community was so much smaller and so intensely networked, minor incidents quickly become known to everyone and panic readily sets in. Another participant, Mingxi (19), was studying at a university located in Melbourne's inner-western suburb of Footscray. When I interviewed Mingxi in Kaifeng, pre-departure, she expressed some unease about stories she had heard that social order was lacking in Footscray, connecting this to that suburb being home to "many Africans and Vietnamese people." However, when, after several months living and studying there, and following the wave of reports about phone thefts by "African gangs," I asked Mingxi whether she was now more worried than before about her personal safety, Mingxi said that she was not. "I'm not scared of Africans," she said. "I mean, you see them in the street in Footscray all the time, but they're fine, they don't do any harm." Such a statement is hardly a shining example of deep inter-cultural exchange and multi-ethnic harmony. However, as Christina Ho observes, the more modest goal of "respecting the presence of others" or "recognition of the other's legitimate presence in a shared social space" can also be seen as an indicator of workable everyday multiculturalism, and may in some cases be a more realistic goal than "harmony" (Ho 2011, 614). Like most media consumers, then, the Chinese students are no cultural dupes: they actively weigh reportage against the evidence of their own experience, and accordingly temper their understanding of and response to social media news and the groups it represents.

Conclusion

In this article, I have tried to show that current conditions of super-diversity in cities like Melbourne mean that we must tailor our approaches to everyday multiculturalism with attention not only to permanent migrants but also to the numerous transient and first-generation migrants ever-present in the city. It is clear that the recently arrived educational migrants who are my focus in this project do not exemplify the deeply hybrid youth cultures found in the 1.5+ generations. Instead, they tend to self-identify as members of a discrete ethnic/ racial, cultural and national group ("Chinese": *Zhongguoren, Huaren*), and in the events I have dealt with here, they tended to figure other groups in a similar way (young men who may have been 1.5 and second-generation African-Australian youth were referred to, often, as "Africans": *Feizhouren / Feiyi* or "black people": *heiren*, while "locals": *dangdiren* was generally reserved for people perceived as white). In the case study above, we have seen class and race working intersectionally to produce particular hostility on the part of the Chinese student community, and its WeChat avatars, toward those perceived to be both "African" *and* "refugees." Despite the geographic proximity of Chinese and African youth in the CBD and Carlton, the quotidian mixing described in many of the neighbour-hood-based everyday multiculturalism studies largely does not occur between these groups. Instead, in the majority of cases, the Chinese students' main encounters with African-heritage youth were via the mediated alarmism of WeChat, while cross-cultural mixing for them occurred primarily with other student groups on university campuses. This stubborn (re)production of social antagonisms based simultaneously in racial and class differentials challenges the assumption that positive urban multicultures can be produced simply by urban proximity.

However, "even" in this case, where arguments based on hybrid ethnic identities cannot gain much purchase, the conflict in question still cannot be seen as the result of ineluctable "ethnic" or "cultural" differences between groups. Rather, it results from the material situation of the communities in question vis-à-vis multiple historico-cultural, socio-economic, micro-political, and media-related factors that (re)produce and exacerbate the Chinese students' tendency to interpret urban space along racialized lines (Park 1996; Amin 2002b; Mankekar 2015, 93–104). Despite the reports from MelToday and other WeChat news accounts repeatedly stating that the phone thefts were principally a case of "African gangs" running rampant, in fact Victoria Police revealed that of 35 arrests made in connection with these crimes, the largest group of arrestees (49 per cent) were white, with only eight "African" and three "African/ Middle East" (together 31 per cent of the total; information released to the author by Victoria Police under the Freedom of Information Act, October 2016). In the case of the tall, dark-skinned youth alleged to have stolen phones from Chinese students, it is not clear which ethnic groups the accused belong to (although it is now clear that, if involved, they formed a minority of offenders). But taking into account the demographic history of African-heritage youth in Melbourne, it is possible that they may have been teenage children of migrants who arrived in Australia through the nation's refugee and humanitarian pro-gramme. If so, then it is clear that their involvement in petty crime will relate to their material situation of social deprivation rather than to essential ethno-cultural characteristics. With regard to responses to the incidents from Melbourne's Chinese student community, although these clearly build on a pre-existing kernel of anti-African racism endemic to modern Chinese culture (Dikötter 1992; Cheng 2011), they, too, were decisively shaped less by ineluctable cultural factors than by economic ones: specifically, the exigencies of minimally regulated ethno-transnational commercial media (Sun 2016).

I have also been arguing that our approaches to everyday multiculturalism need to be enhanced by an appreciation of how people's everyday lives are increasingly shaped by translocal media connections. The ethno-transnational media available to diasporic communities today is qualitatively different to what was available just a decade or so ago and, as I hope my case study has demonstrated, this makes a material difference to the affordances of the media and hence its social impacts, including its impact on how people live with cultural diversity in urban communities. First, new social media like WeChat news accounts are even *more transnational* than older media, insofar as they are accessed from a Chinese platform that allows seamless continuity of use when users travel to Australia. They provide instantaneous, real-time links to people and social life overseas and, as we have seen, their content is also regulated largely from the China end. Second, thanks to mobile-networked technologies, this type of social media is far *more ubiquitous* than older media in everyday life. Eight years ago, Noble suggested that "unpanicked multiculturalism" may flourish in those parts of everyday life that are located "away from the heat of moral panic and [...] media-driven anxieties" (Noble 2009, 51). Yet in the case I have addressed here, where ubiquitous social media became host to a racist moral panic, it seemed at times that for the students involved there *was* no, or precious little, such unmediated part of everyday life where the panic could be avoided (McRobbie and Thornton 1995). Third, these new types of media operate in the wider global context of *intensified deregulation, commercialization, and digital networking of news media*, with attendant risks for the quality of content vis-à-vis journalism's civic function (Fenton 2010; Taylor 2016). Fourth, as a result of a combination of the above factors, this type of media is much more readily able to *evade legal regulation in the host nation*, including evading laws that are aimed at the enhancement of shared social life in multicultural society. Finally, therefore, the example I have addressed highlights the capacity for some forms of new ethno-transnational media, paradoxically, to *undercut multiculturalist values*, as much as to enhance them (Sun 2016). Miyase Christensen and André Jansson propose that "the concept of communication, literally meaning 'making something common,' provides us with a stepping stone for thinking about the relationship between media and cosmopolitanism" (2015, 8). Yet the above examples of WeChat news accounts as a communicative platform encourage what amounts to the opposite effect: not a cosmopolitan engagement, but a hostile turning-away from the (African, refugee) "other" and self-encapsulation within a Chinese (*Huaren*) community that is performatively enacted in repeated references to its self-evident unity of interest. Increased scholarly attention to the role of such new ethno-transnational media in shaping migrants' experiences of cultural diversity – an issue of which this article has only been able to scratch the surface – has the potential to enrich our understanding of how everyday multiculturalism is actually working in Australian (and other) cities under current conditions of intensifying human and media mobility.

It would be unproductive as well as inaccurate to fall back on simplistic arguments that ethno-transnational media like WeChat, as used in Melbourne, are unilaterally harmful to multicultural life, contributing to a "shattered" national public sphere or the erosion of "social cohesion." (Gitlin 1998; Harris 2013; Martin 2016) However, in some limited cases like the one I have presented here, these new media ecologies may throw up new challenges to multicultural living. Our task as scholars of everyday multiculturalism under current conditions of social super-diversity and intensifying transnational connectivity is to tease out how such conflicts are driven by complex underlying webs of material and institutional factors. As the example considered here illustrates, these include, among others, the social and economic distribution of resources and power in the site in question; interplays of commerce and culture shaping available ideological frameworks for people's understandings of cultural difference; and the strain on nation-based civic governance structures in an era when both media and everyday life have become increasingly transnational.

Note

1. This conflation draws on a Chinese racialized imaginary of "the west" as the location of idealized whiteness, which is itself part of the same racialized global imaginary, reaching back to the late nineteenth century, that positions Africanness as "primitive": see discussion above and Dikötter 1992.

Acknowledgement

I gratefully acknowledge the support of the Australian Research Council in providing the funding for the study on which this paper is based. Thanks too to Can Qin, Yuxing Zhou and Juliet Zhou for their invaluable research assistance, and to all of the study participants for generously sharing their experiences with me. I am also grateful to the special issue editors and anonymous reviewers whose feedback was extremely valuable in helping me think through the complex phenomena this article addresses.

Disclosure statement

No potential conflict of interest was reported by the author.

Funding

This work was supported by Australian Research Council [Fellowship number ARC FT140100222].

ORCID

Fran Martin ⓘ http://orcid.org/0000-0003-1265-9577

References

Abur, William. 2012. "A Study of the South Sudanese Refugees' Perspectives of Settlement in the Western Suburbs of Melbourne." Masters thesis (International Community Development), Victoria University.

Amin, Ash. 2002a. "Spatialities of Globalization." *Environment and Planning A* 34 (3): 385–399.

Amin, Ash. 2002b. "Ethnicity and the Multicultural City: Living with Diversity." *Environment and Planning A* 34 (6): 959–980.

Ang, Ien, Jeffrey E. Brand, Greg Noble, and Derek Wilding. 2002. *Living Diversity: Australia's Multicultural Future*. Sydney: SBS.

Bell, Emily. 2016. "The End of the News as We Know It: How Facebook Swallowed Journalism." Tow Center for Digital Journalism at the Columbia Graduate School of Journalism, March 7. https://medium.com/@TowCenter/the-end-of-the-news-as-we-know-it-how-facebook-swallowed-journalism-60344fa50962#.fiab6ge3k.

Bennett, W. Lance. 2004. "Global Media and Politics: Transnational Communication Regimes and Civic Cultures." *Annual Review of Political Science* 7: 125–48.

Bloch, Barbara, and Tanja Dreher. 2009. "Resentment and Reluctance: Working with Everyday Diversity and Everyday Racism in Southern Sydney." *Journal of Intercultural Studies* 30 (2): 193–209.

Cheng, Yinghong. 2011. "From Campus Racism to Cyber Racism: Discourse of Race and Chinese Nationalism." *The China Quarterly* 207: 561–579.

Christensen, Miyase, and André Jansson. 2015. *Cosmopolitanism and the Media: Cartographies of Change*. Houndsmills and New York: Palgrave Macmillan.

Colic-Peisker, Val, and Karen Farquharson. 2011. "Introduction: A New Era in Australian Multiculturalism? The Need for Critical Interrogation." *Journal of Intercultural Studies* 32 (6): 579–586.

Collins, Jock, Carol Reid, and Charlotte Fabiansson. 2011. "Identities, Aspirations and Belonging of Cosmopolitan Youth in Australia." *Cosmopolitan Civil Societies Journal* 3 (3): 92–107.

Cunningham, Stuart. 2001. "Popular Media as Public "Sphericules" for Diasporic Communities." *International Journal of Cultural Studies* 4 (2): 131–147.

Dhanji, Surjeet. 2009. "Welcome or Unwelcome? Integration Issues and the Resettlement of Former Refugees from the Horn of Africa and Sudan in Metropolitan Melbourne." *ARAS* 30 (2): 152–178.

Dikötter, Frank. 1992. *The Discourse of Race in Modern China*. Stanford: Stanford University Press.

Dunn, Kevin, Danielle Pelleri, and Karin Maeder-Han. 2011. "Attacks on Indian Students: The Commerce of Denial in Australia." *Race & Class* 52 (4): 71–88.

Essed, Philomena. 1991. *Understaing Everyday Racism: An Interdisciplinary Theory*. Newbury Park, London and New Delhi: Sage.

Fenton, Natalie. 2010. "Drowning or Waving? New Media, Journalism and Democracy." In *New Media, Old News: Journalism and Democracy in the Digital Age*, edited by Natalie Fenton, 3–16. London: Sage.

Gatt, Krystle. 2011. "Sudanese Refugees in Victoria: An Analysis of Their Treatment by the Australian Government." *International Journal of Comparative and Applied Criminal Justice* 35 (3): 207–219.

Gitlin, Todd. 1998. "Public Sphere or Public Sphericules?" In *Media, Ritual, and Identity*, edited by Tamar Liebes, James Curran, and Elihu Katz, 168–174. London: Routledge.

Harris, Anita. 2013. *Young People and Everyday Multiculturalism*. London and New York: Routledge.

Herbert, Steve. 2016. "Victorian Education Leading the Way in China." Media release from the Victorian Minister for Training and Skills. http://www.premier.vic.gov.au/victorian-education-leading-the-way-in-china/.

Ho, Christina. 2011. "Respecting the Presence of Others: School Micropublics and Everyday Multiculturalism." *Journal of Intercultural Studies* 32 (6): 603–19.

Jinri Chuanmei Jituan 今日传媒集团. 2015. 《今日传媒集团Media Kit 2015》(*Media Today Group Media Kit* 2015), Sydney. http://www.sydneytoday.com/about/contact.html.

Johnson, M. Dujon. 2007. *Race and Racism in the Chinas: Chinese Racial Attitudes Toward Africans and African-Americans*. Bloomington: AuthorHouse.

Mankekar, Purnima. 2015. *Unsettling India: Affect, Temporality, Transnationality*. Durham and London: Duke University Press.

Martin, Fran. 2016. "Media, Place, Sociality, and National Publics: Chinese International Students in Translocal Networks." In *Contemporary Culture and Media in Asia*, edited by Koichi Iwabuchi, Olivia Khoo, and Daniel Black, 209–226. Lanham: Rowman & Littlefield.

Martin, Fran. 2017a. "Rethinking Network Capital: Hospitality Work and Parallel Trading Among Chinese Students in Melbourne." *Mobilities* 12 (6): 890–907.

Martin, Fran. 2017b. "Mobile Self-fashioning and Gendered Risk: Rethinking Chinese Students' Motivations for Overseas Education." *Globalisation, Societies and Education* 15: 706–720.

Martin, Fran, and Fazal Rizvi. 2014. "Making Melbourne: Digital Connectivity and International Students' Experience of Locality." *Media, Culture and Society* 36 (7): 1016–1031.

McRobbie, Angela, and Sarah L. Thornton. 1995. "Rethinking 'Moral Panic' for Multi-mediated Social Worlds." *The British Journal of Sociology* 46 (4): 559–574.

Noble, Greg. 2009. "Everyday Cosmopolitanism and the Labour of Intercultural Community." In *Everyday Multiculturalism*, edited by A. Wise and S. Velayutham, 46–65. Basingstoke and New York: Palgrave Macmillan.

Nolan, David, Karen Farquharson, Violeta Politoff, and Timothy Marjoribanks. 2011. "Mediated Multiculturalism: Newspaper Representations of Sudanese Migrants in Australia." *Journal of Intercultural Studies* 32 (6): 655–671.

Olliff, Louise, and Mohamed. 2007. "Settling in: How Do Refugee Young People Fair within Australia's Settlement System?" Centre for Multicultural Youth Issues, Melbourne. http://cmy.net.au/sites/default/files/publication-documents/Refugee%20Young%20People%20in%20Australia's%20Settlement%20System%202007.pdf.

Park, Kyeyoung. 1996. "Use and Abuse of Race and Culture: Black-Korean Tension in America." *American Anthropologist* 98 (3): 492–499.

Pfafman, Tessa M., Christopher J. Carpenter, and Yong Tang. 2015. "The Politics of Racism: Constructions of African Immigrants in China on China SMACK." *Communication, Culture & Critique* 8: 540–556.

Smith, Michael Peter. 2001. *Transnational Urbanism: Locating Globalization*. Malden: Blackwell Publishing.

Smith, Kerry. 2016. "Media's Racist Post-Moomba Rampage." *Green Left Weekly*, March 17.

Stratton, Jon. 1998. *Race Daze: Australia in Identity Crisis*. Sydney: Pluto Press.

Stratton, Jon. 2006. "Two Rescues, One History: Everyday Racism in Australia." *Social Identities* 12 (6): 657–681.

Sun, Wanning. 2016. *Chinese-Language Media in Australia: Developments, Challenges and Opportunities.* Ultimo: Australia-China Relations Institute.

Tang, Wendy. 2016. "Report: News Consumption Shifts to News Aggregators in China." AllChina Tech, Feburary 11. http://www.allchinatech.com/report-news-consumption-shifts-to-news-aggregators-in-china/.

Taylor, David. 2016. "Social Media Dominates Way Millennials Consume News, Prompting Alarm, Deloitte Survey Says." *ABC News*, August 15. http://www.abc.net.au/news/2016-08-15/social-media-dominates-millenials-consume-news,-deloitte-says/7721528.

Vertovec, Steven. 2007. "Super-diversity and its Implications." *Ethnic and Racial Studies* 30 (6): 1024–1054.

WalkTheChat. 2016. "WeChat Impact Report 2016 is Finally Out!" WeChat official account post, June 26 (via mobile app).

Windle, Joel. 2008. "The Racialisation of African Youth in Australia." *Social Identities* 14 (5): 553–566.

Wise, Amanda. 2005. "Hope and Belonging in a Multicultural Suburb." *Journal of Intercultural Studies* 26 (1-2): 171–186.

Wise, Amanda. 2009. "Everyday Multiculturalism: Transversal Crossings and Working Class Cosmopolitans." In *Everyday Multiculturalism*, edited by A. Wise and S. Velayutham, 21–45. Basingstoke and New York: Palgrave Macmillan.

Wise, Amanda. 2011. "Moving Food: Gustatory Commensality and Disjuncture in Everyday Multiculturalism." *New Formations* 74: 82–107.

Wise, Amanda, and Selvaraj Velayutham. 2009a. *Everyday Multiculturalism.* Basingstoke and New York: Palgrave Macmillan.

Wise, Amanda, and Selvaraj Velayutham. 2009b. "Introduction: Multiculturalism and Everyday Life." In *Everyday Multiculturalism*, edited by A. Wise and S. Velayutham, 1–17. Basingstoke and New York: Palgrave Macmillan.

Worrall, Allison. 2016. "Police Reassure Chinese Students After Wave of Muggings." *The Age*, April 29. http://www.theage.com.au/victoria/police-reassure-chinese-students-after-wave-of-muggings-20160429-goio6d.html.

Humour at work: conviviality through language play in Singapore's multicultural workplaces

Amanda Wise and Selvaraj Velayutham

ABSTRACT

Humour plays an important role in making and mediating human relationships. While scholarship on workplace humour is voluminous, there is scarce literature on interactional humour in non-Western yet culturally diverse settings. This article looks at humour in multi-ethnic Singaporean workplaces employing both citizens and temporary migrants, with a particular focus on blue collar and service workers. We argue that Singlish forms a linguistic and aural humour template for workers to bridge significant language, racial and cultural differences through language play that is devoid of the aggressive disparagement humour that frequently characterizes shop-floor humour in the Anglosphere. What evolves is a humorous metrolingua franca (Pennycook, A., and E. Otsuji. 2015. *Metrolingualism: Language in the City*. London: Routledge.) that is specific to the way everyday multiculturalism operates in diverse Singaporean workplaces.

Humour is a serious business. It plays an important role in making and mediating human relationships, though it is also Janus faced – at once a source[1] of solidarity and a mode of exclusion. Though it is a human universal, interaction humour is deeply situated and specific to small groups. Research shows humour also bears the marks of the wider society and culture from which it derives (Kuipers 2008; Davies 1990). It can bear the marks of gender, race, ethnicity, nation, and class. It is both negotiated and received, mutable and adaptive, yet stubborn in perpetuating negative stereotypes. Interactional humour often involves highly sophisticated social ritual and linguistic play and serves many social functions, sometimes contradictory ones. Social scientists generally agree that it plays a fundamental role in the formation of human sociality and communities. It seems a ripe topic of study, then, for scholars interested in the vicissitudes of everyday multiculturalism and the materialization of new forms of coexistence.

While there have been comparative studies of "joke cultures" around the world (cf Davies 1990, 1982) these have often focused on scripted forms of humour such as jokes and the public humour of comedians, literature and film. Research on interactive forms of humour in culturally diverse non-Western settings is scarcer (see Winkler Reid 2015). Building on a rich tradition of literature on "shop-floor humour" (Collinson 1992, 1988; Korczynski 2011; Willis 2001, 2004) and emerging work on comparative diversities (Wise and Velayutham 2014; Vertovec 2015) this article considers how humour relates to questions of everyday multiculturalism (Wise and Velayutham 2009; Neal et al. 2017). The now substantial body of work on everyday multiculturalism (Wise and Velayutham 2009) or "everyday multiculture" (Neal et al. 2017) considers the nature of and what underpins positive and conflictual inter-ethnic relations at the level of lived experience in quotidian spaces of multicultural encounter such as workplaces, neighbourhoods, schools, leisure spaces and urban streets. This work has explored when and how identities are reconfigured (cf Wessendorf 2014; Noble 2009; Vertovec 2015; Ye 2016) and the nature of cosmopolitanism (as a set of practices, rather than normative ideal) at the vernacular, everyday level. Some of this work also attends to how situations of encounter are shaped by structural and everyday racisms, and variegated conditions of citizenship and migrant legal status and national discourses and architectures of managing and categorizing ethno-racial diversity within the nation-state (Back and Sinha 2016; Neal et al. 2017; Wise 2016a, 2016b; Ye 2016; Vertovec 2015).

In this paper, we explore how humour forms a distinctive modality of everyday multiculturalism in Singapore that draws upon particular characteristics of Singlish as a resource for interacting across cultural and linguistic differences among diverse workers, and consider how Singapore's state policies of migrant labour and multi-racialism inflect these interactions.

The role, effects and function of humour in everyday life have been extensively theorized (Freud 1905; Bergson 1911; Apte 1985; Billig 2005; Kuipers 2008). In locating this study, it is essential to differentiate between different kinds of humour as these entail related though distinct methodologies, empirical foci, and scales and modes of analysis. Formal modes of public humour such as the comedian, TV skit, cartoon, and scripted jokes with a punch-line are the main focus of writers in the critical humour studies tradition (Weaver 2011; Billig 2005; Lockyer and Pickering 2005; Davies 1990). These public humours are distinct – though not unrelated – from interpersonal, interactional modes of humour such as banter, humorous ritual, humour "orgies" (Murphy 2015), "roundings" and put-down humour (Terrion and Ashforth 2002; Plester and Sayers 2007; Murphy 2015, 2017), teasing and ritual insults (Haugh and Bousfield 2012). Interactional humour typically features a kind of "call-and-response" sequence, and a level of reciprocity in the interaction (Kehily and Nayak 1997). Context has a large bearing on the meanings made of humour and the localized power dynamics at play (see Back 1991; Fine 1983), while still being influenced by larger discursive fields.

Most scholars of humour categorize it into three broad theoretical traditions: superiority theory; release theory; and incongruity theory. Various functions of interactional humour have been described. These include humour's role in clarifying and solidifying hierarchical social relationships (Radcliffe-Brown 1940) and gender identities; humour as subversion; dealing with incongruity; establishing boundaries of inclusion and exclusion; easing tension and avoiding conflict, smoothing interactions; saving face and avoiding embarrassment; and forming bonds. Among anthropologists questions of conflict management, ritual and the ludic (Overing 2000) have been central (Roy, Kapferer, Radcliffe- Brown). There are extensive debates on whether "biting humour" (Boxer and Cortés-Conde 1997) can at all be seen as having positive effects. The literature is roughly divided into those who see its value and effects in terms of building social bonds and solidarity, easing tension, marking time, and sometimes subversive effects such as worker resistance; and those who see it largely negative terms, such as Billig (2005; see also Weaver 2011) who argues that all humour is founded upon ridicule and establishing norms of inclusion and exclusion. Most recent work acknowledges that interactional humour functions in both positive and negative ways, even within a single interaction (Kuipers 2008; Wise 2016a). Sociologists in particular have been interested in organizational, shop-floor (Burawoy 1979; Collinson 1992; Willis 1977) and schoolyard humour (Kehily and Nayak 1997). Fine and De Soucey (2005) meditate more generally on the question of what humour *does* for a group. It is instructive that the richest vein of literature in this field is that on workplace humour and within this, banter, teasing, and darker forms of humourous "biting" is predominant. Emblematic here is the work of scholars such as Collinson (1988) on blue collar shop-floor humour, which follows in the tradition of Willis (1977) in its focus on masculinities. What is clear is that humour is an important means of producing and drawing group identities and boundaries, and thus should form an important focus for scholars interested in questions of how ethno-racial difference is lived and experienced in small group settings of a forced encounter, such as culturally diverse workplaces.

We explore these dynamics in multi-ethnic Singaporean workplaces, focusing on the role of humour in how people navigate, reproduce, negotiate and accommodate (or not) linguistic, cultural and "racial" difference at work. Reflecting on emergent forms of intercultural sociality produced through humorous banter and joking activity, this paper considers the following key questions: what do workers in multiethnic workplaces in Singapore joke about and what are the characteristics of interactional humour in these environments? Is cultural and language difference a resource or barrier to shop-floor humour? Is humour enrolled to ease tension and awkwardness around cultural, racial or language difference? How even is the "humour distribution", and is it ever explicitly racist? In addition to the standard reference points of passing time and easing tension, which are well documented in the literature, we show how diverse workers use linguistic and cultural differences as a humour resource to bridge those very differences – and that a certain kind of "language play" involving a distinctive multi-ethnic *metrolingua franca* (Pennycook and Otsuji 2015) is the modality through which this occurs. Overlaying these aspects of function and modality we argue that Singlish forms an overarching humour style which characterizes interactions in Singaporean workplaces.

The study

The paper derives from a larger study on "Everyday Multiculturalism at Work", a mixed-methods comparative project that involved open-ended interviews with workers in Singapore (n.40) and Australia (n.40), and ethnographic observations of workers in Singaporean business parks and food establishments. In Singapore, industries of focus were hospitality sector, retail, shipping, warehousing and hospitals. In Australia: warehouses, hospitals, bus drivers, manufacturing and construction.

The research focused on how culturally diverse blue and pink (service sector) collar workers negotiate ethno-racial differences in their workplaces as lived everyday situations of a forced encounter. We explored how the rules, conditions, codes and rhythms of neoliberal working cultures come to bear on how intercultural encounters are experienced and shaped. Questions and observations were on conflict and bridge building behaviour involving food, language and humour, civilities such as sharing and helping, and incivilities such as discrimination, racism or aggression. The analysis focused on how race, culture, occupational hierarchy, industry, a mix of workers and job style and intensity influenced the shape of everyday inter-ethnic relations at work. The data presented in this paper involves workers in Singapore reflecting on and recounting instances of humour in their diverse workplaces.

Background

Singapore is an immigrant settler city–state with a population of Chinese (74per cent), Malays (14per cent), Indians (10per cent) and "others" (2per cent) (CMIO). These official racial groups have co-existed as discrete, though internally diverse, communities throughout British colonial rule (Goh 2008). Although Singapore experienced racial conflict in the 1950s and 1960s, race relations have remained largely peaceful since independence in 1965. The postcolonial state embarked on a nation-building programme, which included the promotion of economic development, public housing, education and bilingualism, national service, and multiracialism in order to integrate the four races and instil a sense of national identity. People began to cross paths more regularly within housing estates, neighbourhoods, schools and work-places. Nonetheless, with the "four races" CMIO model forming the national template of multi-racial co-existence, interaction has largely been shaped around a state-mediated mode of mixing with "familiar strangers" in highly racialized terms, for example by mandating proportionate racial quotas in the public housing where over 80per cent of Singaporeans reside. Because the Singaporean state – and its colonial predecessor – has so profoundly embedded the language of "race" into all modes of categorization, public policy, inter-communal relations and migration, most Singaporeans use the language of "race" in everyday speech. We use the concept of race parenthetically, recognizing race as a product of racialization rather than a biological construct that has real-world effects (Banton 1998) and thus remains an important focus of analysis.

Coming from vastly different language backgrounds, Malay-, Chinese-, "Eurasian-" and Indian-background Singaporeans evolved a lingua franca by the 1980s. Singlish – colloquial Singaporean English – is characterized by phrases, expressions and words borrowed from Chinese dialects, Malay and Tamil, and humorous language play is a core feature of this local vernacular. Singlish has produced a distinctively Singaporean brand of interactional humour that on the one hand builds on shared experiences and connections (though not intimate) and on the other hand frequently relies on and reinforces racial and cultural stereotypes (cf Goh 2016).

In addition to its citizen population, there is also a growing number of new permanent migrants from the Asian region, especially India, China, and the Philippines, as well as a large number of temporary migrant workers – from elite European and Asian "expats" through to mid-level and low-wage foreign workers from the region. Singapore has a multi-layered differentiated system of temporary visas for overseas workers. At the top of the scale is the "Employment Pass", typically the domain of the white collar professional "expat" classes. Next is the "S-Pass" visa for mid-level skilled workers which employs many Filipinos in the service sector. The pass with most restrictions is the Work Permit, for low wage labourers in construction, cleaning, basic service workers and so forth. There are "source country" requirements by industry and occupation, making the low-end Work Permit (see Figure 1) a highly racialised visa. As a result, class, racial, cultural and religious differences as well as residency status continue to animate everyday social interaction (Velayutham 2009, 2017) in complex ways, including who it throws together at work, and in what ethno-racial concentration.

Domestic Workers	Bangladesh, Hong Kong, India, Indonesia, Macau, Malaysia, Myanmar, Philippines, South Korea, Sri Lanka, Taiwan, and Thailand
Construction	Malaysia People's Republic of China (PRC) Non-Traditional Sources (NTS): India, Sri Lanka, Thailand, Bangladesh, Myanmar and Philippines North Asian Sources (NAS): Hong Kong*, Macau, South Korea and Taiwan.
Service Sector	Malaysia; People's Republic of China (PRC) North Asian Sources (NAS): Hong Kong#, Macau, South Korea and Taiwan.
Marine Sector	Malaysia; People's Republic of China (PRC) Non-Traditional Sources (NTS): India, Sri Lanka, Thailand, Bangladesh, The Republic of the Union of Myanmar and Philippines North Asian Sources (NAS): Hong Kong*, Macau, South Korea and Taiwan.
Process Sector	Malaysia; People's Republic of China (PRC) Non-Traditional Sources (NTS): India, Sri Lanka, Thailand, Bangladesh, Myanmar and Philippines North Asian Sources (NAS): Hong Kong*, Macau, South Korea and Taiwan.
Manufacturing	Malaysia; People's Republic of China (PRC); North Asian Sources (NAS): Hong Kong*, Macau, South Korea and Taiwan.

Figure 1. Work permit approved source countries, by sector.

Singlish as a humour style

"Humour styles" is the term Zijderveld (1983, 1995) uses to describe variations among different national and cultural groups, and these index deep cultural and historical norms (Kuipers 2008, 383). Research on humour styles and scripts also identifies joking themes of universal continuity: sexuality, gender relations, bodily functions, stupidity, and strangers (Apte 1985; cited in Kuipers 2008). Interactional humour is contextual and reflects the cultural idiosyncrasies of people and places, as well as small group cultures (Schnurr and Holmes 2009; Fine 2012). As Fine's (2009) classic study of humour among mushroom collectors has shown, small group cultures frequently employ humour and language scripts that are evolved within and distinctive to the group and are important to the maintenance of group boundaries and identity. Sociolinguists, meanwhile, have developed valuable insights into how humorous linguistic banter works in highly diverse contact zones through concepts such as code switching, code mixing and trans- and poly-lingual languaging. Pennycook and Otsuji's (2015, 3) notion of metrolingual-ism is especially pertinent to our analysis. Metrolingualism describes "the way in which people of different and mixed backgrounds use, play with and negotiate identities through language" and emphasizes the ways in which language is emergent from contexts of interaction. They describe *metrolingua francas* as linguistic practices that draw upon linguistic reper-toires that frequently feature multilingual mixing and borrowing, but evolve out of particular spaces of everyday interaction, which they term spatial reper-toires. Language repertoires occur not just intra-linguistically, and biculturally, but involve very distinctive modalities in very diverse situations of everyday intercultural interaction. The distinguishing feature in our multi-ethnic Singaporean workplaces was a distinctive style of language play, banter and teasing. This involved language borrowing and mixing, using linguistic differences as a resource for humorous engagement across difference, and the frequent use of nicknames and deliberately "silly" uses of familial terms, often borrowing from or playing with these language differences.

Language play – linguistic differences

We argue that that the rhythms and cadences of Singlish form the linguistic and aural template for humorous banter in our Singaporean workplaces and it is used to link not just the four "old races", but in many instances "foreigners" of various backgrounds and migrant statuses. It seemed to be co-opted as a means of dealing with lots of new difference, and is a linguistic style that is particularly adept at accommodating and playing with language and cultural differences.

Language differences frequently served as a source of humour, reflecting the need to get along despite linguistic barriers. Angela recounts a version of the age-old practical joke of teaching a non-speaker vulgarities in your language. Her Chinese supervisor enjoys the practical joke of teaching his Filipino colleague a swear word and suggesting he ask Angela, a Singapore Chinese, what the meaning of the words were.

> My [Filipino] store manager … understands [a little of] our conversation in Mandarin, say, for example, when we say "let's go for our meal." He can repeat that … But … there are instances [where he unwittingly] involved vulgarities. Just the other day, he asked me what a certain word meant. I told him, "Don't learn this. This is a vulgar word. Don't learn." [Laughs.] He said one of the managers taught him that. [Laughs.] Sabo [sabotage]. (Angela, 45, McDonald's crew member, Singapore Chinese)

Siva is a racially Chinese security guard who speaks, comports and culturally identifies as Tamil as he was adopted by a Singaporean Indian family as a baby. He speaks Tamil and English, and a smattering of Chinese and Malay. He talks of feeling a great responsibility to be the joker at his workplace – a large condominium complex that employs about 20 mostly Chinese security guards and a similar number of (largely Malay and Indian) maintenance and cleaning staff on the grounds. His ambiguous racial and cultural identity gives him a certain licence and he likes to entertain his Chinese colleagues by using Mandarin/Chinese dialects in a deliberately amateur way.

> I'm going to ask them "how are you?" But I won't ask them in English. I will make fun in Chinese. So they will be laughing and smiling. So for that also they will

happy. And sometime like, I know how to say "how are you" and *"ni hao ma?"* ["How are you" in Chinese.] But I won't say *"ni hao ma"* in the nicer way. I will say in the funny way, so they will be laughing.

(Siva, 30, Security guard, racially Chinese, adoptee of Singapore Indian family. Speaks Tamil, English, and a little Malay and Mandarin)

In a similar vein, Lhynne – a Filipina IT worker with several Filipino colleagues – recounts how her Singapore Chinese co-workers have learnt key phrases in Tagalog, which they use in a self-deprecatingly humorous way to make fun of their limited ability in this language.

Sometimes they say [in a fun way], *"Gutom ka na ba?* [Are you hungry already?]" They say it in Tagalog, in Filipino language. Or sometimes they say, *"Galit ka ba?* [Are you angry?] ... they speak the language, sometimes they say, *"Ayaw mo ba sa akin sumabay?* [Don't you want to join me?]". Those are some of the jokes because they cannot joke very long messages, just one word. (Lhynne, 37, IT support, Filipina)

Laksmi is a 60-year-old Singaporean Tamil cleaner employed for 17 years by a multinational building firm in one of Singapore's business parks. She is emphatic that humour is the main currency of her workplace existence and it is her humour that makes her an important staff member. She finds it amusing that her Italian boss is bemused at the fact she can understand the unfamiliar accents of the Thai and Burmese workers in their IT and accounts department. The fact that they speak little and also heavily accented English – and Laksmi herself has only marginal English – is not a source of anxiety for her. Indeed, it has become a source of humorous play where they tease each other about their respective accents.

Laksmi:	So many joke. Then sometime the new staff, you know the Filipino, the Thai people, Thai they speak English a bit different. You know, if you say ... sometime I talk to them, they will say "nek wik, nek wik." [Next week]. So "nek wik." So I go and tell the girl, "Eh, nek wik ah, I'm not going to work." "Nek wik." The language is different. Sometime they [Western boss] say "how come you can listen what they say? We cannot you know." "I am local what, that's why I can understand what she said." [Laughs.]
Interviewer:	So the Thai colleagues, they also think it is funny?
Laksmi:	Ya, ya, ya, ya. Sometime I also joke with them, I also make them laugh. "Laksmi, really ah, you like to talk anyhow, make people laugh." "Of course lah. You come office, I see you very sad. Make you laugh-laugh."

Maria, a Filipina working among local and migrant worker Indians in a Little India restaurant recounts a similar example. She seems to see humour as somewhat of a responsibility in her demanding front of house role in her busy Indian eatery.

> ... the thing is, this worker, this chef, they are in a lot of stress. Sometimes you have to cheer them up, you have to joke around. That is one of my job. [Laughs.] Because if they are not happy, the food won't turn out great. Sometimes if they are stressed, so I will joke around. Like I will call him something else in Tagalog. And they would be happy about it. (Maria, 36, hospitality worker, Filipina)

Maria is quite explicit here that it is her duty to "lighten the mood" for the chef because his is an especially stressful job.

Some humour around language difference, though, is less than rosy. Rather than reciprocal and benign banter, there are instances where it was simply ridiculing the language characteristics of a workplace minority. In this case, a 27-year-old male IT administrator recounts how they make fun of the ways in which his Tamil colleagues speak.

> Like one of our HR ... she [teases us], "you know ah, the Filipino is ... " then say it like how we pronounce words, how Filipinos pronounce words ... for Indians [laughs], we just say "yabadubada, yabadubadey", something like that [laughs] because we cannot understand them because the tone of their voice is the same for every words, "yabadubada, yabadubadey". (Mark, 27, IT administrator, Filipino)

Language play is particularly pertinent in multi-lingual blue-collar work places where the use of Singlish and words and expressions from each other's languages help overcome language barriers. Misuse of words, poor and incorrect pronunciations and incomprehensible expressions and accent are turned into moments of playfulness that lubricate social interaction rather than, for the most part, creating conflict or prejudice. Among working class Singaporeans there is little expectation that one should converse in "proper" English. Partial code-switching allows non-proficient English speakers like Angela, Siva and Laksmi to navigate workplace encounters through interactional humour.

Teasing & nicknames

The "Singlish template" for humorous banter was especially present in nick-naming and teasing where languages are mixed, sounds are played upon, or words borrowed. In this example, Kelvin, an electronics store assistant, talks about the nicknames in his workplace.

> [We call the Indian woman] mama safia ... It's like Indian mama like that lah. ... PRCs lah, the [Malays] call them cheena-kueh. Cheena-kueh is the Malay word leh. How to say ah, (in Mandarin from here) tamen jiao women huaren "peh-kueh," baiguo, baiguo [in Mandarin and Hokkien, "They (Malays) call us Chinese 'white cakes.' So cheena-kueh, cheena-kueh. (Kelvin, 35, electronics store assistant, Singapore Chinese)

Mama Safia, for example is probably a mispronunciation of the Tamil *Sappediya?* meaning "have you eaten" – a very common motherly Tamil phrase – referring to the fact that this is one of her stock phrases of greeting in the workplace. *Cheena kueh* is a play on the term for a type of sweet Malay snack and refers to the relatively light skin colour of Chinese people. Food analogies are a familiar humour trope in Singapore – particularly the use of food names to the reference body, skin colour and other racial markers. Maria, the Filipina hospitality worker, likes to playfully use terms her Hindi-speaking chef does not understand, then tell him later what it actually means.

> Sometimes the [chef], I call him *"lolo." "Lolo"* means grandfather [in Tagolog]. [Laughs] And if he asks me, *"'lolo'* means what?" "It means 'handsome.'" [Laughs] And then at the end of the day I would tell him the meaning. [Laughs] And then, "what's the word for 'grandmother' in Filipino?" Then I told him, *"lola."* Then he call me *"lola."* [Laughs]. (Maria, 36, hospitality worker, Filipina)

This is typical of the gender teasing we found, where "handsome" or "pretty" in one language is used – usually in the language of the joker, or across age groups – playing on the incongruity involved.

> Sometimes we would call [our male Filipino colleagues] *"aunty"* jokingly. For the Malaysian, we call him *leng zai* ["handsome" in Cantonese].

> … He would call us 'aunty', or *leng ma* [Cantonese, for "pretty mama"] … When things get busy and he needs us to work faster, he would call us *leng ma* sweetly. [Laughs] And sometimes we call him (the Malaysian) *suay zai* … It's like … a child who cannot follow instructions lah in Cantonese. [Laughs] … Ya, we joke around quite a bit. (Siew Lin, older woman, McDonald's crew, Singapore Chinese)

Sometimes a play on familial-, age- or gender-related terms is used – such as a Filipino male calling his similar aged Singapore-Chinese colleague "aunty". Siew Lin also mentions using Cantonese nicknames for her Malaysian colleague.

The choice of words and phrases and the way they are pronounced and peppered in conversations by a non-native speaker was a key source of humour. The humour lies in the clumsy usage and the surprise it produces (e.g. a Chinese person knowing some Tamil or a Malay/Tamil person speaking Mandarin). This becomes even more pronounced when non-Singaporeans such as Anglo, Filipino, Burmese, Thai workers, use Singlish exclamations like *lah, alamak, aiyah* in their sentences. Other examples like "aunty", "uncle", *mamak, makcik, abang* [2] help to establish a level of informality and conviviality. Though not explicitly humorous as such, this generates some humour when used by a non-native speaker. This applies even to an Indian calling a Chinese woman "aunty" – an attempt to smooth over language differences. Often these are the only terms an individual will know in their colleague's language.

Channel Five – easing tension, passing time

Many theorists and ethnographers identify passing time and easing tension as key functions of humour (cf Kuipers 2008; Fine and De Soucey 2005; Roy 1959). These themes were frequently highlighted by our interviewees. One running joke we heard about in several workplaces involved how Singaporeans, especially Malay and Tamil minorities, respond to ease the awkwardness of being left out of a conversation due to language barriers. In such instances, they would call out in a humorous way "Channel 5 Please!" – a reference to one of Singapore's English-language television channels – so that the group discussion switches to English. This is a well-known joke in Singapore that has also been adapted to other versions in the workplaces we studied. For example Priya, a 40-year-old Tamil airline ground staff for Singapore Airlines jokingly remonstrates her Chinese colleagues that "this is not China Airlines" if they speak Chinese in front of her. This also works the other way around, with Chinese colleagues reminding her, "this is not Indian airlines":

> P: Sometimes at work right, don't like them talking in Chinese, for instance. [I'll say jokingly] "This is not the China Airlines, but Singapore Airlines". So you just tell them, okay, speak in English. … And even when they talk in Tamil I've got colleague who will say, "Wah, Indian Airlines." Ya. (Priya, 40 year old female Tamil. Airline ground staff)

In such instances, humour is used to deal with an otherwise uncomfortable experience of feeling language-excluded – but the joke needs to be understood by all parties for it to play its "tension-easing role" (Wise 2016a). Nadeera, a 35-year-old Malay nurse, has a rather more restrained view than Maria and Priya. She says that "Singaporeans" get this joke correctly because they grew up with it, but "foreigners" – Filipina and PRC nurses, don't know that joke and continue speaking in their language, which she finds insulting:

> Ok. This is common because we have been in a multi-racial society [in Singapore] since we in school. So for example when you are with your Chinese friends and they see you coming in and they are having a conversation, they will say "Eh, please switch to Channel Five" (switch to English Language). But for the foreigners, from my personal view, they are not as sensitive as our locals. They will just carry on until you have to ask them what they are talking about, then only will they tell you. Our Singaporeans, they are more sensitive. (Nadeera, 35yo Female Malay nurse.)

In this case, Singapore's "in-joke" – commonly understood as a means of expressing an otherwise awkward request – is invoked as a marker of

Singaporean identity itself. Velayutham (2017) has argued that for long-time Singaporeans, multi-racial and multi-cultural accommodation is in itself seen as reflective of a national cultural habitus that defines the essence of being a Singaporean. Nadeera's account can be read both in straightforward terms, but also as a microcosm of this identity dynamic.

Numerous studies on work temporalities show humour can play a key role in dealing with accelerated work intensities (Flaherty 2011) as well as the "beast of monotony" (Roy 1959) that long working days and unstimulating jobs can invoke. In Siew Lin's workplace, teasing centres on managing potentially tense times in a busy work schedule where communication breaks down because of language differences. She recounts the hilarity of having to hold up picture cards to get the PRC Chinese cook to identify which burger they have just handed over:

> The jokes. [Laughs] … They are really funny sometimes … they [PRC Chinese colleagues] are preparing the burger, and they cannot pronounce the name correctly in English. … So I held up the sheet with the names and diagrams, and asked if it is this patty with this sauce and bun. They don't know the proper names in English. They haven't been here for long, the ones from China. So they could not tell the burgers apart. There are so many different kinds of chicken burgers! [Laughs]. (Siew Lin, older woman, McDonald's crew, Singapore Chinese)

Cindy, another McDonalds crew member, talks animatedly about the fact there are Singapore Malays, Malaysian Malays and Tamils, as well as Filipinos, Singapore Chinese and PRC Chinese at her workplace and what an enormous social achievement it is that they manage not only to get their job done, but to do so with a level of conviviality that brings some degree of pleasure to an otherwise low-paid, low-status job. She speaks with amazement and some level of pride that they mostly get on very well, and that even though they do not understand a lot of what one another have to say, they manage by gesture, by learning words here and there, and she places humour at the centre of how this is dealt with.

> They also … like a duck and a chicken (and still try to manage to make sense despite speaking in different languages). My managers are Filipinos. Then my aunties (or crew), like Siew Lin, she works with a Filipino crew. She can still, "ya, ya, ya, ya" and the Filipino will also "ya, ya, ya, ya." They can still somehow manage to get their messages across.

Noor, a Singapore-Malay security guard, suggests that the main role of humour at her place of employment is fundamentally important in relieving the sheer tedium of her work.

> [We] joke around sometimes [with the Malaysian Indians], not that bored ah. [So we don't get bored] You see the same face you know? [How] Can we not

joke? [Laughs] Without the joke, I cannot lah. Like that, I die. (Noor, 26, security guard, Singapore Malay)

Siva, introduced earlier, sees this as a kind of service to his workplace, and as a form of self-therapy.

> If I think about my own problem, and sit one corner, I will go mad. So don't put your problem first, put your problem aside, go and disturb people, make fun of them, go and play with them, talk-talk, chit-chat. So you will be forgetting your problem.

> ….That's you know, whoever around me, or around us, you make them laugh or happy ah, it's considered a good deed. I believe that lah. Medicine, a kind of medicine also ah. (Siva, 30, security guard)

Laksmi also feels a sense of recognition from her colleagues that she has developed the reputation for being the person to make everyone laugh, to cheer them up when someone seems flat. Like Siva, she also suggests that this makes herself feel better.

> Ya, everybody will laugh. Sometime my staff office say, "I'm so sad, Laksmi. Anything joke? Tell me anything joke." Anything, bad things or what, I will tell. Then after that will say "I'm so happy now, …. Myself, even if I sad, I still like to make them laugh. Make me myself happy also. (Laksmi, 60, cleaner, Singapore Tamil)

Lakshmi's account highlights the mutual and reciprocal convivial labour that goes into these humour interactions. In this light, humour does not necessarily arise from positive collegiality but is constitutive of it (see Wise 2016a).

Discussion and conclusions

Our findings fit within several of the classic functional categories identified in the sociological humour studies literature (cf Kuipers 2008, 2009, 2015; Fine 1983). The relevance of "release theory" in the stories around "passing time and easing tension" is clearly applicable. We can also see that much of the humour involving borrowing and twisting of language plays on incongruity (Apte 1985), and much of the humour work revolves around easing the potential tension of having to function in a workplace where there are significant language barriers. There are also instances of subversion of authority where superiors have nicknames behind their backs (Collinson 1988). We can see the ritual nature of some of the humour (Roy 1959) and the use of irony (Winkler Reid 2015). These are all reasonably straightforward findings. However, there is one thing that stands out when comparing the style of humour we found in our research among male blue-collar Australian workplaces (Wise 2016a),[3] and the humour in Singaporean workplaces. What is apparent is the absence of "hard" disparagement humour that was present in our Australian workpalces, and the extent to which language differences served as a resource for humour in Singapore, but not in Australia. What accounts for this difference?

There is a rich tradition of research on shop-floor humour in the Anglo-sphere (Burawoy 1979; Collinson 1992; Willis 1977) and much of this work takes questions of white working class masculinity as a central focus. From the 1990s important work began to emerge tracking how humour manifests differently in feminine workplaces. Some researchers have found that there are distinctive features of feminine workplace humour that differ markedly from the combative humour displays elaborated by Willis, Collinson and others in their studies of male blue-collar workplaces. Korczynski, Pickering, and Robertson (2013, 250) argue that humour used in masculine cultures tends to be more competitive and aggressive and can lead to a spiral of dis-integrating community, whereas in feminine shop-floor cultures, humour tends to be used in communally more supportive ways. We argue that not only is humour gendered, it is cultured. And, we suggest, it is "cultured", even when it is "multi-cultured".

Humour forms an important resource in the workings of Singaporean everyday multiculturalism. Because humour requires the participation of the micro-group, the style and content of the humour will reflect, not only the cul-tural orientations of individual group members. It also gains its collective "groove" from the larger societal context in which it occurs. This explains, in the Australian data, the fact that in more masculine industries, there is a level of co-optation of "multicultural others" into an Anglo-male shop-floor humour style that has a long history (See Wise 2016a). It is adapted and makes accommodations at the edges, yet the "template" of white male blue-collar masculine humour forms the predominant style at the local group level. Whereas we found that in very diverse workplaces without a sig-nificant Anglo majority, the humour style was more accommodative and ten-tative in feeling towards the limits of humour acceptability. In other words, the humour patterns reflect the cultural styles of both individuals and their own cultures as well as the wider culture.

Singapore was more reflective of the latter dynamic, enabled by Singa-pore's postcolonial lingua franca, Singlish. As we have argued, Singlish forms a linguistic and rhythmic template for humorous banter that works across cultural and language differences. As Goh points out

> given its origins, its status as an alternative to standard languages and its func-tion as a lingua franca, Singlish … has a fundamentally basic and earthy charac-ter, suited much more to expressing practical everyday realities, and as emotional intensifiers, than abstract ideas (2016, 749).

Singlish lends itself to amusing language accommodation, code switching, mixing and negotiation and Singaporeans have developed an ear for gram-matical shortcuts and mixing of expressions and languages. They are accustomed to using and adjusting their English / Singlish when interacting with those with whom they do not fully share a language and there is comparatively little anxiety about not sharing a language. Even when the humour exchange is not specifically Singlish, we suggest it still forms a background template for humorous exchanges with linguistic "Others" – both Singaporean and newer migrants from completely or partially different language backgrounds. Humour draws on these linguistic "muddling alongs" and often plays on accommodating and borrowing across languages, making light of gaps in language understanding. We also find that many non-Singaporeans become socialized into this humorous language game.

Everyday multiculturalism needs to be understood as an analytic that sees interaction as occurring in, yet transcending, "the situation", where encounters are shaped by more than the everyday. Pratt's notion of the contact zone describes the "social spaces where cultures meet, clash, and grapple with each other, often in contexts of highly asymmetrical relations of power, such as colonialism, slavery, or their aftermaths" (1991, 34). It reminds us that power and history is never absent, even in the most convivial situations of encounter. Comparing "everyday multiculturalism" in a non-Western context highlights how national differences (structural and cultural) do matter, even at the most local levels of day-to-day encounter. While in Australia and elsewhere in the Anglosphere, a lack of or marginal English is frequently a basis for exclusion and racism, Singapore's history of language mixing and general ability to transact across linguistic differences offers a different kind of dominant "template" into which diverse workers can find a collective "groove". It works not just across Singapore's four "CMIO races", as many of the humour scripts are familiar to South and Southeast Asian "foreigners" as well. In this way, Singlish forms the basis of a kind of convivial labour (Wise 2016a; Noble 2009) that diverse workers employ to facilitate he business of multi-ethnic forced co-existence at work. At the same time the nature of work and the stratified and racialized system of work visas, sort Singaporean workers in complex ways that has a bearing on the "thickness" of interaction across difference and frames some groups as first and foremost members of a particular national group (see Wise 2016b). These visas have a bearing on who works with whom in what industry, and the level of ethno-racial "clustering" of workers from particular countries. We found more fluid interactions in the upper mid-range technical (S-Pass) and white collar jobs (Employment Pass) for example – due to the much more mixed nature and less racialized nature of the migrant worker employment passes in these workplaces. This contrasted with the workplaces where there were many Work Permit holders, on the extremely precarious and racially stratified lowest form of temporary work visa. Conversely, we found little evidence of Tamil migrant workers included in humour interactions, suggesting that the Southeast Asian / Singapore Chinese humour style offers an ambivalent form of inclusion to racialised Tamil workers. While Singlish involves multilingual mixing and borrowing, it is heavily inflected with Chinese dialects. As recent scholarship on "Chinese privilege" in Singapore attests (Velayutham 2017), the terms of national inclusion more generally are tilted to Chinese Singaporean advantage.

In conclusion, it is important to emphasize that everyday racial tensions, and indeed outright racism, are not uncommon in Singapore. In a context of a majority Chinese population, the racial minorities and migrant workers have to work harder to establish convivial relations from a, frequently from a standpoint of precarious inclusion. So while "convivial labour" (Wise 2016a, Wise and Noble 2016) is at the heart of all forms of successful co-existence, this labour is not evenly distributed. As familiar strangers (Ye 2016), Singaporeans and migrant workers have the social licence to connect and interact with one another, not unproblematically, through the invocation of racial stereotypes as well as shared and affectionate cultural tropes. Here Singlish bridges the social distance between the various races, enveloping them in an interactional mode of co-existence, and these tropes and modalities of interacting across difference become the template upon which newer migrant "Others" are co-opted into this global city.

Notes

1. See Kuipers (2008) for a comprehensive review of the literature on humour in sociology.
2. Rough Singlish translations: *Abang* (elder brother), *alamak* (oh my goodness /my God); *aiyah/aiyoh* (oh bugger / damn/ expressive of frustration); *lah* (commonly appended to the end of words for humorous emphasis); *Mamak* (uncle) *Makcik* (younger aunt).
3. Humour in our Australian workplaces is discussed and theorized at length in Wise (2016b).

Disclosure statement

No potential conflict of interest was reported by the authors.

Funding

This study was supported by the Australian Research Council [grant number DP120101157]

References

Apte, M. 1985. *Humour and Laughter: An Anthropological Approach*. New York: Cornell University Press.

Back, L. 1991. "Social Context and Racist Name Calling: an Ethnographic Perspective on Racist Talk Within a South London Adolescent Community." *The European Journal of Intercultural Studies* 1 (3): 19–38.

Back, L., and S. Sinha. 2016. "Multicultural Conviviality in the Midst of Racism's Ruins." *Journal of Intercultural Studies* 37 (5): 517–532.

Banton, M. 1998. *Racial Theories*. Cambridge: Cambridge University Press.

Bergson, H. 1911. *Laughter: An Essay on the Meaning of the Comic*. London: Macmillan Co.

Billig, M. 2005. *Laughter and Ridicule: Towards a Social Critique of Humour*. Thousand Oaks: Sage.

Boxer, D., and F. Cortés-Conde. 1997. "From Bonding to Biting: Conversational Joking and Identity Display." *Journal of Pragmatics* 27 (3): 275–294.

Burawoy, M. 1979. *Manufacturing Consent*. Chicago: Chicago University Press.

Collinson, D. L. 1988. "'Engineering Humour': Masculinity, Joking and Conflict in Shop-Floor Relations." *Organization Studies* 9 (2): 181–199.

Collinson, D. L. 1992. *Managing the Shopfloor: Subjectivity, Masculinity and Workplace Culture*. Berlin: Walter de Gruyter.

Davies, C. 1982. "Ethnic Jokes, Moral Values and Social Boundaries." *The British Journal of Sociology* 33 (3): 383–403.

Davies, C. 1990. *Ethnic Humor Around the World: A Comparative Analysis*. Bloomington: Indiana University Press.

Fine, G. A. 1983. "Sociological Approaches to the Study of Humor." In *Handbook of Humor Research*, 159–181. New York: Springer.

Fine, G. A. 2009. *Morel Tales: The Culture of Mushrooming*. Cambridge: Harvard University Press.

Fine, G. A. 2012. "Group Culture and the Interaction Order: Local Sociology on the Meso-Level." *Annual Review of Sociology* 38: 159–179.

Fine, G. A., and M. De Soucey. 2005. "Joking Cultures: Humor Themes as Social Regulation in Group Life." *Humor - International Journal of Humor Research* 18 (1): 1–22.

Flaherty, M. G. 2011. *The Textures of Time: Agency and Temporal Experience*. Philadelphia: Temple University Press.

Freud, Sigmund. 1905. *Jokes and Their Relations to the Unconsciousness*. Harmondsworth: Penguin.

Goh, D. P. 2008. "From Colonial Pluralism to Postcolonial Multiculturalism: Race, State Formation and the Question of Cultural Diversity in Malaysia and Singapore." *Sociology Compass* 2 (1): 232–252.

Goh, R. B. 2016. "The Anatomy of Singlish: Globalisation, Multiculturalism and the Construction of the 'Local' in Singapore." *Journal of Multilingual and Multicultural Development* 37 (8): 1–11.

Haugh, M., and D. Bousfield. 2012. "Mock Impoliteness, Jocular Mockery and Jocular Abuse in Australian and British English." *Journal of Pragmatics* 44 (9): 1099–1114.

Kehily, M. J., and A. Nayak. 1997. "'Lads and Laughter': Humour and the Production of Heterosexual Hierarchies." *Gender and Education* 9 (1): 69–88.

Korczynski, M. 2011. "The Dialectical Sense of Humour: Routine Joking in a Taylorized Factory." *Organization Studies* 32 (10): 1421–1439.

Korczynski, M., M. Pickering, and E. Robertson. 2013. *Rhythms of Labour: Music at Work in Britain*. New York: Cambridge University Press.

Kuipers, G. 2008. "The Sociology of Humor." In *The Primer of Humor Research*, edited by V. Raskin, 361–398. Berlin: Walter de Gruyter.

Kuipers, G. 2009. "Humor Styles and Symbolic Boundaries." *Journal of Literary Theory* 3 (2): 219–239.

Kuipers, G. 2015. *Good Humor, Bad Taste: A Sociology of the Joke*. Berlin: Walter de Gruyter.

Lockyer, S., and M. Pickering. 2005. *Beyond a Joke: the Limits of Humour*. London: Palgrave.

Murphy, S. P. 2015. "Humor Orgies as Ritual Insult Putdowns and Solidarity Maintenance in a Corner Donut Shop." *Journal of Contemporary Ethnography*. doi:0891241615605218

Murphy, S. P. 2017. "Humor Orgies as Ritual Insult: Putdowns and Solidarity Maintenance in a Corner Donut Shop." *Journal of Contemporary Ethnography* 46 (1): 108–132.

Neal, S., K. Bennett, A. Cochrane, and G. Mohan. 2017. *Lived Experiences of Multiculture: The New Social and Spatial Relations of Diversity*. London: Routledge.

Noble, G. 2009. "Everyday Cosmopolitanism and the Labour of Intercultural Community." In *Everyday Multiculturalism*, edited by A. Wise, and S. Velayutham, 46–65. Houndsmills: Palgrave Macmillan.

Overing, J. 2000. "The Efficacy of Laughter." In *The Anthropology of Love and Anger: the Aesthetics of Conviviality in Native Amazonia*, edited by Joanna Overing, and Alan Passes, 64–81. London: Routledge.

Pennycook, A., and E. Otsuji. 2015. *Metrolingualism: Language in the City*. London: Routledge.

Plester, B. A., and J. Sayers. 2007. "'Taking the Piss': Functions of Banter in the IT Industry." *Humour – International Journal of Humour Research* 20 (2): 157–187.

Pratt, M. L. 1991. "Arts of the Contact Zone." *Profession* 33–40.

Radcliffe-Brown, A. R. 1940. "On Joking Relationships." *Africa* 13 (03): 195–210.

Roy, D. 1959. "'Banana Time': Job Satisfaction and Informal Interaction." *Human Organization* 18 (4): 158–168.

Schnurr, S., and J. Holmes. 2009. "Using Humor to do Masculinity at Work." In *Humor in Interaction*, edited by N. R. Norrick and D. Chiaro, Vol. 182, 101–124. Vancouver: John Benjamins Publishing.

Terrion, J. L., and B. E. Ashforth. 2002. "From 'I' to 'we': the Role of Putdown Humor and Identity in the Development of a Temporary Group." *Human Relations* 55 (1): 55–88.

Velayutham, S. 2009. "Everyday Racism in Singapore." In *Everyday Multiculturalism*, edited by A. Wise and S. Velayutham, 255–273. Houndsmills: Palgrave Macmillan.

Velayutham, S. 2017. "Feels so Foreign in my own Homeland': Xenophobia and National Identity in Singapore." In *Precarious Belongings: Affect and Nationalism in Asia*, edited by Chih-Ming Wang, and Daniel P.S. Goh, 153–168. London: Rowan & Littlefield International.

Vertovec, S., ed. 2015. *Diversities Old and New: Migration and Socio-Spatial Patterns in New York, Singapore and Johannesburg*. London: Springer.

Weaver, S. 2011. *The Rhetoric of Racist Humour: US, UK and Global Race Joking*. Burlington: Ashgate Publishing.

Wessendorf, S. 2014. *Commonplace Diversity: Social Relations in a Super-Diverse Context*. London: Springer.

Willis, P. 1977. *Learning to Labour*. London: Saxon House.

Willis, Paul. 2001. "Tekin'the Piss." In *History in Person: Enduring Struggles, Contentious Practice, Intimate Identities*, 171–216. Oxford: James Curry.

Willis, P. 2004. "Shop Floor Culture, Masculinity and the Wage Form." In *Feminism and Masculinities*, edited by Peter F. Murphy, 108. Oxford: Oxford University Press.

Winkler Reid, S. 2015. "Making Fun Out of Difference: Ethnicity – Race and Humour in a London School." *Ethnos* 80 (1): 23–44.

Wise, A. 2016a. "Convivial Labour and the 'Joking Relationship': Humour and Everyday Multiculturalism at Work." *Journal of Intercultural Studies* 37 (5): 481–500.

Wise, A. 2016b. "Becoming Cosmopolitan: Encountering Difference in a City of Mobile Labour." *Journal of Ethnic and Migration Studies* 42 (14): 2289–2308.

Wise, A., and G. Noble. 2016. "Convivialities: An Orientation." *Journal of Intercultural Studies* 37 (5): 423–431.

Wise, A., and S. Velayutham. 2009. *Everyday Multiculturalism*. Houndsmills: Palgrave Macmillan.

Wise, A., and S. Velayutham. 2014. "Conviviality in Everyday Multiculturalism: Inhabiting Diversity in Singapore and Sydney." *European Journal of Cultural Studies* 17 (4): 406–430.

Ye, J. 2016. "The Ambivalence of Familiarity: Understanding Breathable Diversity Through Fleeting Encounters in Singapore's Jurong West." *Area* 48 (1): 77–83.

Zijderveld, A. 1983. *Reality in a Looking Class: Rationality through the Analysis of Traditional Folly*. London: Routledge Kegan & Paul.

Zijderveld, A. C. 1995. "Humor, Laughter, and Sociological Theory." *Sociological Forum* 10 (2): 341–345.

Index

Note: Page numbers followed by "n" refer to notes.

Allport, G. W. 69
Amin, Ash 57, 69
Ang, I. 11, 12
attentiveness 70, 71, 75–78, 81
Aziz, N. A. 17

Baig, Raees 5, 6
Berger, Peter 53
Billig, M. 107

care ethics approach 67–83
caregiving 71
caring about 70
caring for 70–71
Channel Five 115–117
Chinese University of Hong Kong 56
Christensen, Miyase 101
Collinson, D. L. 107, 118
Committee on the Promotion of Racial
    Harmony (CPRH) 51–52
competence 71, 75–77, 79, 81
contact hypothesis 69
conviviality 13, 14, 20, 25, 64, 69, 120;
    community 61, 62; interethnic 11;
    through language play 105–120
cosmopolitan consumption 23
CPRH see Committee on the Promotion of
    Racial Harmony
cultural diversity 3–5, 22, 30, 33, 35, 41,
    43, 44, 68, 70, 72, 88, 91, 100
Cunningham, Stuart 95–96

De Soucey, M. 107
Dikötter, Frank 91–92, 101n1
discrimination 19, 39, 40, 49, 52, 55, 60,
    67, 73, 108; institutional 48; racial 51
division of labor 61, 81

doing of care 70–72
Dreher, Jochen 53, 54
Durkheim, Emile 61

eldercare in Singapore, multicultural
    landscapes of 72–75
Equal Opportunities Commission 50
Essed, Philomena 88
ethnicity 11, 14, 17, 18, 21, 26, 31, 39, 43,
    55–57, 63, 71, 72, 93, 94; see also racism
everyday cosmopolitanism 21–23
everyday multiculturalism: in/across Asia
    2–4; in Malaysia 13–14; in Melbourne
    88–91; in multiracialized Malaysia
    10–26; 1Malaysia and 15–17; power
    in 53–54; in union 48–64; see also
    individual entries
everyday otherness 31, 37, 42, 44,
    60; power through negotiating,
    reconstruction of 58–59
everyday pragmatics 23–24
everyday racism 5, 106; in Malaysia 11, 13,
    14, 17–19, 25; in Melbourne 88–91; in
    South Korea 31, 34, 44

FADWU see Federation of Asian Domestic
    Workers' Unions
Federation of Asian Domestic Workers'
    Unions (FADWU) 49, 57, 58, 62, 63
Ferrarese, M. 21, 22
Fine, G. A. 107, 110
formal spaces of integration 19–21
Freedom of Information Act 99

Gabriel, S. P. 14
Gastmans, C. 82n1
Goh, R. B. 108

Grant, Carl A. 35
Green, B. 72, 82n1

Halberstam, J. J. 80
Ham, Sejung 35
Han, Alan 5
Harris, Anita 5, 15, 31
HKCTU see Hong Kong Confederation of
    Trade Unions
HKDWGU see Hong Kong Domestic
    Workers General Union
HKSAR see Hong Kong Special
    Administrative Region
Hong Kong 49; Basic Law, Article 26, 51;
    Census and Statistics Department 51;
    Employment Ordinance 50; Federation
    of Asian Domestic Workers' Unions 49;
    Immigration Ordinance 50; Section
    2(4) 51; International Domestic
    Workers Federation 53; live-in policy
    67; New Condition of Stay policy 51;
    Standard Employment Contract (ID
    407) 50; transnational female labour
    movement: exclusion from the policy
    formulation on multiculturalism
    51–52; Nepalese MDWs, multiple
    vulnerabilities of 52–53; social and
    political exclusion 50–51; 2-week rule
    50, 51; Union of Nepalese Domestic
    Workers in Hong Kong 53
Hong Kong Confederation of Trade
    Unions (HKCTU) 49, 53, 56–58, 62, 63
Hong Kong Domestic Workers General
    Union (HKDWGU) 56, 58
Hong Kong Special Administrative Region
    (HKSAR) 51, 52
Huang, Shirlena 5, 6
humour at work 105–120; background
    108–110; Channel Five 115–117;
    Singlish, as a humour style 110–115;
    language play 111–113; teasing &
    nicknames 113–115; study 108
hybridity 18, 25, 89–90

IDFW see International Domestic Workers
    Federation
incongruity theory 107
Indonesia 49
International Domestic Workers
    Federation (IDFW) 53, 56
Ismail, N. A. 17

Jansson, André 101
Jones, H. 21
Joseph, C. 23

Khoo, G. C. 22, 25
Korczynski, M. 118
Krauss, S. E. 20
Kuipers, G. 120n1

labour solidarity, equalling power
    through 60–61
Lachman, V. D. 77, 82n1
language play 6, 108, 109, 111–113, 117
learning to care across cultures,
    possibilities and limits in 75–81; failed
    unmakings 80–81; limited remaking
    78–80; transformative possibilities
    76–77
Leong, C.-H. 25
Lian, Kwen Fee 3
Luckmann, Thomas 53

Malaysia: "Bangsa Malaysia" (or
    "Malaysian race") policy 25; everyday
    cosmopolitanism 21–23; everyday
    multiculturalism in 3, 13–14; everyday
    pragmatics 23–24; everyday racism
    in 17–19; formal spaces of integration
    19–21; "Malaysia, Truly Asia" campaign
    13; MCIO classification system 14,
    18; multiculturalism in 11–13; New
    Economic Policy 12; 1Malaysia 5, 10–26
Martin, Fran 6
McDonalds 21
MDWs see migrant domestic workers
Melbourne's Chinese student world,
    everyday racism and ethno-
    transnational media in 86–101; modern
    Chinese public culture, race and
    Africanness in 91–92; phones, gangs,
    and WeChat 92–98
MelToday 97
metrolingua franca 108, 110
migrant domestic workers (MDWs):
    unionism, power construction in
    48–64; framework 54–55; power in
    everyday multiculturalism 53–54;
    power through labour solidarity,
    equalling 60–61; power through
    negotiating everyday otherness,
    reconstruction of 58–59; research
    methodology 55–57; transnational
    female labour movement 50–53; union,
    as space for cross-ethnic interaction 57
mixophilia 68
mixophobia 68
modern Chinese public culture, race and
    Africanness in 91–92
multicultural co-living 3

multiculturalism: everyday (*see* everyday multiculturalism); exclusion from the policy formulation on 51–52; in Malaysia 11–13; without diversity, limits of 29–44

neoliberal approach to eldercare 72–73
Nepalese MDWs, in Hong Kong 55, 56, 59; multiple vulnerabilities of 52–53
nicknames 113–115
Noble, Greg 36, 38, 42, 89, 100
Noor, N. M. 25
North America: everyday multiculturalism in 2, 3
nursing homes in Singapore, multicultural encounters in 67–83; care ethics 70–72; doing of care 70–72; eldercare 72–75; learning to care across cultures, possibilities and limits in 75–81

1Malaysia (1M) 5, 10–26; and everyday multiculturalism 15–17
openness 13, 15, 59, 68, 70, 80
otherness/othering 34, 36, 39, 40, 43, 61, 64; everyday 31, 37, 42, 44, 60; power through negotiating everyday otherness, reconstruction of 58–59
Otsuji, E. 110

Pennycook, A. 110
Philippines 49
Pickering, M. 118
political exclusion of migrant domestic workers 50–51
polyethnic neighbourhood 89
power: in everyday multiculturalism 53–54; through labour solidarity, equalling 60–61; through negotiating everyday otherness, reconstruction of 58–59
Pratt, M. L. 119

Race Daze (Stratton) 88
racism: everyday 5, 106; in Malaysia 11, 13, 14, 17–19, 25; in Melbourne 88–91; in South Korea 31, 34, 44; South Korea: "difference" and experiences of racism, tensions of 34–37; *see also* ethnicity
Radford, David 37, 60
Raghuram, P. 72, 75, 80–81
Razak, Najib Tun 12, 25
relationality 68, 71
release theory 107
responsibility 70–71, 75–79, 81

responsiveness 71, 75–77, 79, 81
Robertson, E. 118

Salleh, S. M. 22
schema of perception 42
Scuzzarello, S. 71
Semi, G. 14
separatism 14, 19
Shan, Hongxia 61
Singapore: CMIO policy 73, 108, 109; everyday multiculturalism in 3; humour at work 105–120; background 108–110; Singlish, as a humour style 110–115; study 108; intercultural encounters in 68–70; nursing homes, multicultural encounters in 67–83; care ethics 70–72; doing of care 70–72; eldercare 72–75; learning to care across cultures, possibilities and limits in 75–81
Singlish, as a humour style 110–115; language play 111–113; teasing & nicknames 113–115
skilful resistance 40–43
sociability 3, 13; multicultural 82
social cohesion 101
The Social Construction of Reality 53, 54
social exclusion of migrant domestic workers 50–51
sociality 13; human 105; intercultural 107
South Korea: everyday multiculturalism in 3; schools, multi-ethnic students and the negotiation of "difference" in 29–44; "difference" and experiences of racism, tensions of 34–37; methodology 31–34; positionality 33–34; skilful resistance 40–43; strategic invisibility 37–39
state, formulation of the multiculturalism policy by 53
strategic invisibility 37–39
Stratton, Jon 88
super-diversity 6, 67, 89, 90, 98, 101
superiority theory 107
Survey and Behavioural Research Ethics Faculty Sub-committee of the Faculty of Social Sciences 56

Tamam, E. 20, 24
teasing 113–115
transformative possibilities of learning to care 76–77
transversal enablers 55, 61, 62, 64
Trinity College Foundation Studies Program 86
Tronto, J. C. 70–72, 78, 81, 82n1

UNDW *see* Union of Nepalese Domestic
　Workers in Hong Kong
union, as space for cross-ethnic
　interaction 57
Union of Nepalese Domestic Workers in
　Hong Kong (UNDW) 53, 56, 58, 63
United Nations Committee on the
　Elimination of Racial
　Discrimination 52

Valentine, G. 69
Vanlaere, L. 82n1
Velayutham, Selvaraj 6, 13, 116
Vertovec, Steven 67, 89, 90

Walter, Pierre 61
Walton, Jessica 5
Watkins, Megan 41
WeChat 86, 91–101
Willis, Paul 107, 118
Wilson, H. F. 80, 81
Wise, Amanda 6, 13, 55, 61, 69, 120n3

Yazid, M. Y. 17
Yeoh, Brenda 5, 6
"Young People and Social Inclusion in the
　Multicultural City" 15

Zijderveld, A. C. 110